A GUIDE TO

MUCH ADO ABOUT NOTHING

The Shakespeare Handbooks

Guides available now:

- Antony and Cleopatra
- As You Like It
- The Comedy of Errors
- Cymbeline
- Hamlet
- Henry IV, Part 1
- Julius Caesar
- King Lear
- Macbeth
- Measure for Measure
- The Merchant of Venice
- The Merry Wives of Windsor
- A Midsummer Night's Dream
- Much Ado About Nothing
- Othello
- Richard II
- Romeo and Juliet
- The Tempest
- Twelfth Night
- The Winter's Tale

Further titles in preparation.

The Shakespeare Handbooks

A Guide to
Much Ado About Nothing

by Alistair McCallum

Upstart Crow Publications

First published in 2020 by
Upstart Crow Publications

Copyright © Alistair McCallum 2020

A CIP catalogue record for this book
is available from the British Library

ISBN 978 1 899747 17 7

www.shakespeare-handbooks.com

Setting the scene

Shakespeare wrote *Much Ado About Nothing* in 1598–9, when he was in his mid thirties. Having started his career as a novice actor ten years or so before, he was by now the principal playwright for London's leading theatre company; his achievements to date included *Richard II, Romeo and Juliet* and *A Midsummer Night's Dream*. He and his fellow company members were soon to set up the renowned Globe Theatre on the south bank of the Thames.

Much Ado About Nothing seems to have been an immediate and continuing success with the theatre-going public. It was a favourite at the royal court, too, and King James I, who came to the throne in 1603, commissioned several private performances.

The play remained popular until, with civil war looming, the theatres were forced to shut down in 1642; they were to remain closed for nearly twenty years. By the time they reopened, tastes had changed radically. As happened with many other Shakespeare plays, characters and scenes were lifted from *Much Ado* and combined with parts of other plays, along with music and dancing, to create elaborate performances designed to appeal to a supposedly more refined public. Eventually, however, the original play became popular once more, and it has remained a firm favourite to this day.

Much Ado is a fast-paced comedy of wit and rivalry. Its language is sparkling and assured, and its plot, driven by eavesdropping, deception and misunderstanding, is masterfully controlled. But the play challenges us with hints of darkness, even tragedy, before giving us the happy conclusion that we desire:

"Shakespeare offers a play of light and dark, of romantic union wrested from fear and malice, and of social harmony soothing the savagery of psychic violence. Much Ado *claims one of Shakespeare's most delightful heroines, his most dancing word-play, and the endearing spectacle of intellectual and social self-importances bested by the desire to love and be loved in return. It is undoubtedly the most socially and psychologically realistic of his comedies, in its portrait of the foibles and generosities of communal life."*

Claire McEachern, Introduction to the Arden Shakespeare edition of *Much Ado About Nothing*, 2006

The conflict comes to an end

The prince of Aragon, Don Pedro, has been dealing with an armed rebellion. He has succeeded in defeating the rebels, and the fighting is over.

Don Pedro is now on his way to Messina, a coastal city in the Aragonese territory of Sicily. While there, he plans to celebrate his victory and enjoy an extended stay at the home of Leonato, the governor of Messina.

Curtain up

Encouraging news

The governor of Messina, Leonato, is waiting outside his house with his daughter Hero and his niece Beatrice, anxious for news of the recent conflict.

A messenger from the victorious prince Don Pedro arrives to tell the governor that the prince and his companions are now on their way to Messina. Leonato is relieved to hear that casualties have been light:

Leonato: How many gentlemen have you lost in this action? [1]
Messenger: But few of any sort, and none of name. [2]
Leonato: A victory is twice itself when the achiever brings home full numbers.

[1] *battle*
[2] *distinction, nobility*

As Leonato reads the letter brought by the messenger, he notices that a particular young man has been singled out for praise:

Leonato: I find here that Don Pedro hath bestowed much honour on a young Florentine called Claudio.
Messenger: Much deserved on his part, and equally remembered [1] by Don Pedro. He hath borne himself beyond the promise of his age, [2] doing, in the figure of a lamb, the feats of a lion ...

[1] *suitably acknowledged and rewarded*
[2] *he has shown more valour than would be expected of such a young man*

Leonato mentions that Claudio has an uncle in Messina. The messenger replies that he has already visited the man, who was overcome with pride to hear of his nephew's bravery. Such displays of emotion are a mark of good character, Leonato believes:

Leonato: Did he break out into tears?
Messenger: In great measure.

Leonato: A kind[1] overflow of kindness: there are no faces truer
              than those that are so washed. How much better is it
              to weep at joy than to joy at weeping!

[1] *natural, instinctive*

Beatrice makes her feelings known

Beatrice asks the messenger whether her acquaintance
Benedick is among those coming to Messina with the prince.
She remarks that his talent is for gluttony rather than warfare:

Messenger: He hath done good service, lady, in these wars.
Beatrice: You had musty victual,[1] and he hath holp[2] to eat it:
             he is a very valiant trencherman;[3] he hath an excellent
             stomach.

[1] *stale food*
[2] *helped*
[3] *hearty eater, man of good appetite*

Leonato assures the messenger that Beatrice's sarcasm should
not be taken too seriously. When they are together, she and
Benedick continually attempt to outdo one another with their
cutting remarks, he explains. Beatrice claims that she always
gets the better of him:

Leonato: You must not, sir, mistake my niece. There is a kind
              of merry war betwixt Signior Benedick and her: they
              never meet but there's a skirmish of wit between them.
Beatrice: Alas, he gets nothing by that. In our last conflict four
              of his five wits[1] went halting off,[2] and now is the whole
              man governed with one: so that if he have wit enough
              to keep himself warm, let him bear it for a difference
              between himself and his horse[3] ...

[1] *the five wits were considered to be imagination,*
    memory, common sense, fantasy and instinct
[2] *limped away, unable to carry on*
[3] *he should hold on to his one remaining wit, as it is*
    the only thing that distinguishes him from a beast

According to Beatrice, Benedick is fickle, continually shifting his loyalty from one friend to another:

Beatrice: Who is his companion now? He hath every month a new sworn brother.

Messenger: Is't possible?

Beatrice: Very easily possible: he wears his faith but as the fashion of his hat, it ever changes with the next block.[1]

Messenger: I see, lady, the gentleman is not in your books.[2]

Beatrice: No; an[3] he were, I would burn my study.

[1] *wooden mould for shaping hats, replaced whenever fashions change*
[2] *is not in your good books; does not meet with your approval*
[3] *if*

Benedick's best friend, the messenger says, is Claudio, the young man commended in Don Pedro's letter for his bravery. Beatrice sympathises with him. Benedick's company will prove to be a disaster, she claims:

Beatrice: O Lord, he will hang upon him like a disease; he is sooner caught than the pestilence,[1] and the taker[2] runs presently[3] mad. God help the noble Claudio!

[1] *the plague*
[2] *victim, infected individual*
[3] *immediately*

*... he is sooner caught than the pestilence, and the
taker runs presently mad.*

There are numerous mentions of the plague throughout Shakespeare's work. The plague was a constant source of anxiety, particularly for those who made their living from the theatre. When a severe epidemic occurred in London – defined as more than 30 deaths a week – the theatres were closed down by the authorities who believed, probably correctly, that large public assemblies helped to spread the disease. Unfortunately for the theatre companies, epidemics tended to happen during the summer, when the theatres – which had no lighting or heating – did most of their business.

It was not only in London that the plague cast its shadow. In Shakespeare's home town it had wiped out almost one in six of the population in the course of a few terrible months in 1564. The newborn Shakespeare was lucky to survive unscathed:

"Plague was a frequent and devastating occurrence in England throughout Shakespeare's lifetime. Those who contracted it could suffer from fevers, delirium, and painful plague sores, with a survival rate of just 50%. In 1564, the year Shakespeare was born, plague claimed over 200 people in Stratford-upon-Avon, including four children on his very street. The ominously brief and simple statement 'hic incepit pestis' ('here begins the plague') was written in the burial register at Stratford's Holy Trinity Church on the 11th of July; Shakespeare had been baptised there less than three months before ... The persistent presence and threat of this fearsome disease should not be forgotten when considering Shakespeare's life and works."

Holly Kelsey, *Pestilence and Playwright*, 2016

The adversaries meet

Prince Don Pedro now arrives. Among his companions are Benedick and Claudio, his comrades-in-arms in the conflict that has just ended. Leonato greets the visitors warmly.

When Don Pedro is introduced to Hero, the governor's daughter, Leonato takes the opportunity to tease Benedick about his reputation as a libertine:

Don Pedro: ... I think this is your daughter.
Leonato: Her mother hath many times told me so.
Benedick: Were you in doubt, sir, that you asked her?
Leonato: Signior Benedick, no, for then were you a child.[1]
Don Pedro: You have it full, Benedick; we may guess by this what you are, being a man.[2] Truly the lady fathers herself.[3] Be happy, lady, for you are like an honourable father.

[1] *at the time of her conception, you were not old enough to be a father*
[2] *Leonato has answered your question perfectly, and summed up your character*
[3] *Hero's similarity to Leonato is ample evidence that he is her father*

Benedick remarks that Hero would not wish to resemble her grey-haired father too closely. As the others drift away, Beatrice addresses him mockingly. Benedick bemoans the fact that she seems to be the only woman who does not admire him – not, he adds, that he is particularly interested in female company:

Beatrice: I wonder[1] that you will still be talking, Signior Benedick: nobody marks you.[2]
Benedick: What, my dear Lady Disdain! Are you yet living?[3]
Beatrice: Is it possible disdain should die, while she hath such meet[4] food to feed it as Signior Benedick? Courtesy itself must convert to disdain,[5] if you come in her presence.

Benedick: Then is courtesy a turncoat.[6] But it is certain I am loved
of all ladies, only you excepted; and I would I could
find in my heart that I had not a hard heart, for truly I
love none.

[1] *I'm surprised*
[2] *is taking any notice of you*
[3] *still alive*
[4] *suitable, ideal*
[5] *even the most polite of people must become scornful*
[6] *traitor*

It is just as well that Benedick is not seeking to ensnare a woman in a relationship, declares Beatrice. She too finds the idea of romance unbearable:

Beatrice: … I thank God and my cold blood, I am of your humour
for that;[1] I had rather hear my dog bark at a crow than a
man swear he loves me.

[1] *my temperament is the same as yours in that respect*

"Much Ado About Nothing *features the most obviously modern of Shakespeare's courting couples, Beatrice and Benedick. They are the direct ancestors of the 'rom-com' couple ... Despite there being some examples of witty banter between young men and women in earlier Shakespeare plays and in some other 16th-century texts, Beatrice and Benedick are definitively new: they refuse to abide by the conventions of genteel decorum, they know their own minds (or think they do), they are not particularly respectful of authority ... Perhaps their banter is also a type of self-defence against the appearance of any emotional vulnerability."*

Penny Gay, *Benedick and Beatrice: the 'merry war' of courtship*, 2016

Don Pedro, having spoken briefly to Leonato, announces that he and his companions have been invited to stay in Messina, at the governor's house, for at least a month.

Leonato, confirming the invitation, turns to Don Pedro's illegitimate brother, Don John. There has been hostility between the prince and his brother, a taciturn, sullen individual, but now that the quarrel is over Don John is an honoured guest:

Leonato: Let me bid you welcome, my lord, being reconciled to the Prince your brother: I owe you all duty.

Don John: I thank you: I am not of many words, but I thank you.

Claudio is smitten

As the assembled company leaves for Leonato's house, Claudio takes Benedick aside. He wants his friend's opinion of Leonato's daughter Hero:

Claudio: Benedick, didst thou note the daughter of Signior Leonato?

Benedick: I noted her not,[1] but I looked on her.

Claudio: Is she not a modest young lady?

[1] *I did not pay particular attention to her*

To Claudio's frustration, Benedick refuses to take the subject seriously. She may be moderately attractive in her way, he suggests vaguely, but she does not live up to his idea of beauty:

Claudio: … I pray thee speak in sober judgement.

Benedick: Why, i' faith, methinks she's too low[1] for a high praise, too brown[2] for a fair praise, and too little for a great praise: only this commendation I can afford her, that were she other than she is, she were unhandsome,[3] and being no other but as she is,[4] I do not like her.

[1] *short*
[2] *brown-haired, dark*
[3] *she would be unattractive if she looked different*
[4] *since she is the way she is*

Benedick is concerned that his friend has become infatuated, and may make a rash decision. He can think of at least one woman who is far more beautiful than Hero, although her temperament makes her company unbearable:

Claudio: In mine eye, she is the sweetest lady that ever I looked on.

Benedick: I can see yet[1] without spectacles, and I see no such matter: there's her cousin, an she were not possessed with a fury,[2] exceeds her as much in beauty as the first of May doth the last of December. But I hope you have no intent to turn husband, have you?

[1] *still*

[2] *if she were not possessed by a ferocious demon*

Don Pedro now comes out to ask the two men what they have been discussing so earnestly, and why they have not joined the company in Leonato's house. Ignoring Claudio's plea for secrecy, Benedick immediately reveals the truth; that his friend has fallen in love with Hero.

At first, Claudio is reluctant to admit that he is in love, but with the prince's encouragement he soon makes his feelings clear. Don Pedro strongly approves of the match, but Benedick remains unenthusiastic, and mocks his friends' solemn declarations:

Claudio: That I love her, I feel.

Don Pedro: That she is worthy, I know.

Benedick: That I neither feel how she should be loved, nor know how she should be worthy, is the opinion that fire cannot melt out of me; I will die in it at the stake.

Although Benedick does not hold a grudge against women in general, he does not intend to let himself become ensnared by a woman who, in time, will no doubt prove unfaithful. Indeed, the constant threat of infidelity makes marriage intolerable for both husband and wife, he claims, so it is safer to avoid it altogether.

Don Pedro believes that Benedick's attitude will change in time:

Benedick: That a woman conceived me, I thank her: that she
brought me up, I likewise give her most humble
thanks ... Because I will not do them the wrong to
mistrust any,[1] I will do myself the right to trust none:
and the fine[2] is, for the which I may go the finer,[3] I will
live a bachelor.

Don Pedro: I shall see thee, ere I die, look pale with love.

Benedick: With anger, with sickness, or with hunger, my lord, not
with love ...

[1] *I will not insult any woman by putting her in a
situation where I will mistrust her*
[2] *conclusion*
[3] *which will leave me richer, and free to spend more
money on fine clothes*

Don Pedro light-heartedly warns Benedick that his outspoken criticism of marriage will make him a figure of fun when he finally succumbs to love. Benedick remains steadfast. If he were ever to marry, he insists, he would deserve to be ridiculed in public: he is unworried, however, as he is confident that it will never happen.

An indirect approach

Benedick leaves for Leonato's house, and Claudio, alone with Don Pedro, reveals the strength of his feelings. He had been aware of Hero before leaving Messina for the recent war, but it is only since his return that the depth of his fondness for her has suddenly become clear. The prince is amused by the young man's poetic, extravagant language:

Claudio: ... now I am return'd, and that war-thoughts
Have left their places vacant, in their rooms[1]
Come thronging soft and delicate desires,
All prompting me[2] how fair young Hero is,
Saying I lik'd her ere I went to wars.

Don Pedro: Thou wilt be like a lover presently,
And tire the hearer with a book of words.

[1] *in their place*
[2] *reminding me, making me realise*

Claudio admits that he wants the prince's help in proposing to Hero, and in obtaining Leonato's blessing for the marriage of his only child. Don Pedro mentions that there is to be a masked ball this evening, in celebration of the recent victory. He offers to approach both Hero and her father, and win them over to the idea of the marriage:

> *Don Pedro:* ... I will assume thy part[1] in some disguise,
> And tell fair Hero I am Claudio,
> And in her bosom I'll unclasp my heart,[2]
> And take her hearing prisoner with the force
> And strong encounter of my amorous tale:
> Then after to her father will I break,[3]
> And the conclusion is, she shall be thine.
>
> [1] *take on your role; pretend to be you*
> [2] *open my heart, reveal my true feelings*
> [3] *broach the subject*

Eager to put the plan into practice, the two men leave to prepare for the ball.

A misunderstanding

I, ii

Leonato is in his house, busily organising the evening's festivities, when his brother Antonio arrives with some surprising news. A servant, he reports, has overheard part of a conversation between Don Pedro and Claudio. However, the man has misinterpreted the prince's plan:

> *Antonio:* The prince and Count Claudio, walking in a thick-pleached[1] alley in mine orchard, were thus much overheard by a man of mine: the prince discovered[2] to Claudio that he loved my niece your daughter, and meant to acknowledge[3] it this night in a dance ...
>
> [1] *lined with dense, intertwined branches*
> [2] *disclosed, revealed*
> [3] *declare, affirm*

It seems that Don Pedro, in short, intends to propose to young Hero. The servant is completely trustworthy, Antonio insists, but Leonato remains cautious. He is not sure whether the story is true, but decides that Hero should have her answer ready all the same:

Leonato: … we will hold it[1] as a dream till it appear itself:[2] but I will acquaint my daughter withal,[3] that she may be the better prepared for an answer, if peradventure this be true.[4]

[1] *regard the idea*
[2] *materialises, proves genuine*
[3] *with what you have told me*
[4] *in case it turns out to be true*

> *"Much Ado's central plot device is the readiness of the characters to accept error and misinformation ... The theme of error and confusion is also enhanced by various other dramatic devices. Prominent is the repeated importance of overhearing, an act that lends itself to misinterpretation and error ... The very title of the play may contain a pun on this subject, for 'nothing' was probably pronounced like 'noting', which in Elizabethan English could mean 'overhearing' or 'eavesdropping'."*
>
> Charles Boyce, *Shakespeare A to Z*, 1990

Lingering hostility

Elsewhere in Leonato's house, the prince's brother Don John is in conversation with his companion Conrade. Unlike his brother, Don John is a surly, unfriendly individual; and at the moment he is in a particularly resentful mood. Conrade encourages him to raise his spirits, but Don John refuses to conceal his unhappiness. He will be himself, he insists, regardless of other people's feelings:

> *Don John:* I cannot hide what I am: I must be sad when I have
> cause, and smile at no man's jests; eat when I have
> stomach,[1] and wait for no man's leisure;[2] sleep when
> I am drowsy, and tend on no man's business;[3] laugh
> when I am merry, and claw no man in his humour.[4]
>
> [1] *appetite*
> [2] *never wait until others are ready*
> [3] *ignore anyone else who wishes to deal with me*
> [4] *not flatter anyone by showing sympathy*

It emerges that Don John played a part in the recent rebellion against Don Pedro. Conrade warns him that he will need to hide his bitterness if he is to benefit from the prince's goodwill:

> *Conrade:* … you must not make the full show of this till you may
> do it without controlment.[1] You have of late stood out[2]
> against your brother, and he hath ta'en you newly into
> his grace,[3] where it is impossible you should take true
> root but[4] by the fair weather that you make yourself.
>
> [1] *you must not show your resentment until you are free*
>   *to do so without restraint*
> [2] *rebelled, plotted*
> [3] *recently taken you back into his favour*
> [4] *except*

Don John remains defiant: he refuses to make a dishonest show of benevolence or gratitude. He may have been pardoned, but he does not feel as if he has been given his freedom. Although he cannot express his anger openly, as he would like, it is still there:

Don John: I had rather be a canker[1] in a hedge than a rose in his grace ... in this, though I cannot be said to be a flattering honest man, it must not be denied but I am a plain-dealing villain. I am trusted with a muzzle and enfranchised with a clog[2] ... If I had my mouth[3] I would bite; if I had my liberty I would do my liking: in the meantime, let me be that[4] I am, and seek not to alter me.

[1] *wild rose*
[2] *like a dangerous dog, I am only trusted when wearing a muzzle, and only set free with a heavy weight around my leg*
[3] *if my muzzle were removed*
[4] *what*

Another of Don John's companions, Borachio, now enters. The evening's festivities are starting, he reports. He has been employed to perfume the rooms in Leonato's house, and this enabled him, unexpectedly, to overhear a surprising conversation between Don Pedro and Claudio.

Don John, who despises Claudio for his part in defeating the recent rebellion, senses a possible opportunity:

Borachio: Being entertained for a perfumer,[1] as I was smoking a musty room comes me[2] the prince and Claudio, hand in hand in sad conference.[3] I whipped me behind the arras,[4] and there heard it agreed upon that the prince should woo Hero for himself, and having obtained her, give her to Count Claudio.

Don John: Come, come, let us thither; this may prove food to my displeasure. That young start-up hath all the glory of my overthrow.[5] If I can cross him any way, I bless myself every way.

[1] *hired to freshen the rooms by burning bunches of sweet-smelling herbs*
[2] *towards me, into my presence*
[3] *serious conversation*
[4] *wall-hanging, tapestry*
[5] *the young upstart has gained his honour by defeating me*

Don John sets off with his companions to join the party, determined to cause trouble for Claudio and disrupt his plans if he possibly can.

Shakespeare wrote *Much Ado About Nothing* in his mid thirties, during a period of intense activity and creativity. He had been an actor for several years, but by this time he had also become a hugely successful playwright. This success must have gone hand in hand with a hectic lifestyle:

"In the Elizabethan repertory system, Shakespeare might be expected to perform in six different plays on six consecutive days. Many times he would rehearse one play in the morning and perform in another that afternoon. On most days he probably played more than one character ... When he was not acting in plays he was writing them. Like actors, Elizabethan playwrights were encouraged to demonstrate their adaptability. In less than twenty-four months at the turn of the seventeenth century Shakespeare wrote Much Ado About Nothing, The Life of Henry the Fifth, The Tragedy of Julius Caesar, As You Like It, *and* The Tragedy of Hamlet Prince of Denmark, *probably in that order, probably one right after the other. Even before he finished one play he had begun thinking about or even writing the next ..."*

Gary Taylor, *Reinventing Shakespeare*, 1989

Anticipation

Leonato, host of the victory celebrations, is waiting, with his family, for Don Pedro and the other guests to arrive. He asks whether Don John is present, but no one has seen him. Beatrice remarks how aloof and gloomy the man is:

Beatrice: How tartly[1] that gentleman looks! I never can see him but I am heart-burned an hour after.[2]

Hero: He is of a very melancholy disposition.

Beatrice: He were an excellent man that were made just in the mid-way between him and Benedick: the one is too like an image[3] and says nothing, and the other too like my lady's eldest son, evermore tattling.[4]

[1] *sour, disagreeable*
[2] *without having indigestion for an hour afterwards*
[3] *picture or statue*
[4] *too much like a spoilt mummy's boy, always chattering foolishly*

The talk quickly turns to marriage. Leonato playfully warns his niece that her mischievous attitude will frighten off admirers:

Leonato: By my troth,[1] niece, thou wilt never get thee a husband, if thou be so shrewd[2] of thy tongue.

[1] *I assure you*
[2] *sharp, critical*

Leonato and his brother Antonio believe, mistakenly, that Don Pedro will propose to Hero this evening. They remind her that she is expected to give a favourable response. Beatrice interrupts, urging Hero to refuse her suitor if she is unsure:

Antonio: [*to Hero*] Well, niece, I trust you will be ruled by your father.[1]

Beatrice: Yes, faith, it is my cousin's duty to make curtsy and say, 'Father, as it please you': but yet for all that, cousin, let him be a handsome fellow, or else make another curtsy and say, 'Father, as it please me'.

Leonato:	... Daughter, remember what I told you: if the Prince do solicit you in that kind,[2] you know your answer.

[1] *accept your father's instructions*
[2] *raises the subject of marriage as we discussed*

Hearing the guests approach, Leonato and the others put on their masks in preparation for the ball. Don Pedro, Benedick and Claudio, also masked, now make their entrance, along with Don John, Borachio and the rest of the guests.

The musicians strike up, and the dancing begins.

Private conversations

As the dance progresses, the masked participants mingle, and soon separate into couples. The anonymity offered by the masks provides an opportunity for flirtation and light-hearted conversation, and the first to make a move is Don Pedro. He identifies Hero, as planned, and asks her to dance. She responds encouragingly, but teases him about the ugliness of his mask:

Don Pedro:	Lady, will you walk a bout[1] with your friend?
Hero:	So[2] you walk softly, and look sweetly, and say nothing, I am yours for the walk; and especially when I walk away.[3]
Don Pedro:	With me in your company?
Hero:	I may say so, when I please.
Don Pedro:	And when please you to say so?
Hero:	When I like your favour, for God defend[4] the lute should be like the case!

[1] *take part in this dance*
[2] *as long as*
[3] *even when I move away from you*
[4] *God forbid*

Leonato's brother Antonio approaches Ursula, one of Hero's attendants, but his disguise is ineffective:

Ursula: I know you well enough, you are Signior Antonio.
Antonio: At a word,[1] I am not.
Ursula: I know you by the waggling of your head.
Antonio: To tell you true, I counterfeit him.[2]
Ursula: You could never do him so ill-well,[3] unless you were the very man.

[1] *in a word, in short*
[2] *I'm pretending to be him*
[3] *imitate his faults so perfectly*

Antonio's dry, wrinkled hand reveals his age, Ursula points out. She consoles him by assuring him that it is his keen wit that truly gives him away.

Beatrice and Benedick are dancing together, though she is unaware of his identity. As they talk, he reveals that someone has been criticising her behind her back, though he cannot say who. Beatrice is outraged, and can guess who the culprit is:

Beatrice: Will you not tell me who told you so?
Benedick: No, you shall pardon me.[1]
Beatrice: Nor will you not tell me who you are?
Benedick: Not now.
Beatrice: That I was disdainful, and that I had my good wit out of the 'Hundred Merry Tales'[2] – well, this was Signior Benedick that said so.
Benedick: What's he?
Beatrice: I am sure you know him well enough.
Benedick: Not I, believe me.

[1] *if you'll forgive me; if you don't mind*
[2] *a popular collection of unsophisticated jokes and comic stories*

Beatrice paints an unflattering picture of Benedick for the benefit of her unknown partner:

Beatrice: Why, he is the Prince's jester, a very dull fool; only his gift is in devising impossible slanders.[1] None but libertines [2] delight in him …

Benedick: When I know the gentleman, I'll tell him what you say.

Beatrice: Do, do, he'll but break a comparison or two on me,[3] which peradventure not marked,[4] or not laughed at, strikes him into melancholy …

[1] *his only skill lies in thinking up ridiculous insults*
[2] *idle, shallow individuals*
[3] *he'll only make a couple of ineffective, scornful comments about me*
[4] *if they happen to be ignored*

"In Much Ado *Shakespeare explores the powers and pleasures of speaking well. The dialogue is formal, mannered and elegant, but also enlivened by the well-turned phrase, the quick retort, and the punch-line, governed by the tension between the decorous and the daring. Conversation is both a dance and a form of combat … we have the sense of being in the presence of a kind of everyday eloquence, all the more enviable because seemingly effortless."*

Claire McEachern, Introduction to the Arden Shakespeare edition of *Much Ado About Nothing*, 2006

An easy target

Don John, loitering at the edge of the celebrations, has noticed that his brother Don Pedro has taken Leonato aside for a confidential exchange.

Knowing of Claudio's love for Hero, and the prince's plan to arrange their marriage, Don John decides to take action. He spots a lone masked figure, and Borachio confirms that it is Claudio. Don John approaches, pretending to have mistaken him for Benedick. Claudio plays along with the error. However, he is dismayed when Don John mentions, disapprovingly, that an engagement is imminent:

Don John:	Are you not Signior Benedick?
Claudio:	You know me well, I am he.
Don John:	Signior, you are very near my brother in his love.[1] He is enamoured on[2] Hero; I pray you, dissuade him from her, she is no equal for his birth.[3] You may do the part of an honest man in it.[4]
Claudio:	How know you he loves her?
Don John:	I heard him swear his affection.
Borachio:	So did I too, and he swore he would marry her tonight.

[1] *you are a close friend of the prince*
[2] *in love with, infatuated with*
[3] *beneath him, of inferior status*
[4] *it would be the act of a loyal friend*

Left alone, Claudio reflects bitterly on his mistake in trusting Don Pedro. The prince clearly wanted Hero for himself and has, inevitably, put his own desires ahead of their friendship:

Claudio:	Thus answer I in name of Benedick,
	But hear these ill news with the ears of Claudio.
	'Tis certain so; the Prince woos for himself.
	Friendship is constant[1] in all other things
	Save[2] in the office[3] and affairs of love ...

[1] *faithful, unchanging*
[2] *except*
[3] *business*

Claudio reproaches himself unhappily; he should have known that this might happen. While he is brooding on his loss, Benedick approaches. Believing, like Claudio, that Don Pedro is engaged to Hero, he sympathises with the young man. He does not regard his friend's loss as particularly serious, however, and Claudio leaves, uninterested in his friend's light-hearted comments.

It now becomes clear what is on Benedick's mind. He is still smarting from the words that Beatrice – not realising who her partner was – used to describe him while they were dancing. The idea that he is regarded as a jester is intolerable; it must be Beatrice's own perverse opinion, he decides, not that of the world in general. He resolves to get even with her:

> *Benedick:*   … that my Lady Beatrice should know me, and not know me![1] The Prince's fool! Ha! It may be I go under that title because I am merry. Yea, but so I am apt to do myself wrong.[2] I am not so reputed: it is the base, though bitter, disposition of Beatrice that puts the world into her person, and so gives me out.[3] Well, I'll be revenged as I may.
>
> [1] *should be acquainted with me, yet fail to understand my true character*
> [2] *if I believe that, I am doing myself a disservice*
> [3] *Beatrice's mean, heartless nature makes her imagine that the world shares her low opinion of me, and so she falsely portrays my reputation in that way*

"To the Elizabethan the most degraded of all forms of wit … was that of the professional fool, or jester, who in his worst form was known as the ale-house jester. By the end of the 16th century he was the one type of professional jester that was almost universally condemned and in the most indignant terms, particularly as one who misled young gentlemen, nobles, and princes. His jests were not mere second-hand tales and more or less stupid retorts; they were scurrilous, degraded, and vicious …"

Charles Baskervill, *The Quarrel of Benedick and Beatrice*, 1917

Harmony restored

Don Pedro now arrives, and Benedick rebukes him for (as he believes) taking Claudio's sweetheart. He compares the prince to a schoolboy who steals a bird's nest that his friend has shown him.

To Benedick's relief, Don Pedro makes it clear that, as promised, he has been encouraging Hero to marry Claudio, not attempting to win her himself:

Benedick: ... the rod he might have bestowed on you, who, as I take it, have stolen his bird's nest.

Don Pedro: I will but teach them to sing, and restore them to the owner.[1]

Benedick: If their singing answer your saying, by my faith you say honestly.[2]

> [1] *I just want to make sure that the two lovers are in agreement, and then I will leave them to carry on with their courtship*
>
> [2] *if they speak to one another lovingly, as you describe, then you are clearly telling the truth*

Don Pedro informs Benedick that Beatrice has a bone to pick with him. She too was stung by their exchange during the dance. Although she was unaware of the identity of her partner, she assumed that the insults he mentioned originated with Benedick.

Benedick defends himself vociferously, insisting that he had suffered unbearable verbal abuse:

Don Pedro: The Lady Beatrice hath a quarrel to you. The gentleman that danced with her told her she is much wronged by you.

Benedick: O, she misused me past the endurance of a block![1] ... She told me, not thinking I had been myself,[2] that I was the prince's jester, that I was duller than a great thaw,[3] huddling jest upon jest with such impossible conveyance upon me that I stood like a man at a mark,[4] with a whole army shooting at me. She speaks poniards,[5] and every word stabs.

[1] *her criticism was so harsh that even an inanimate object could not have endured it*
[2] *not realising who I was under the mask*
[3] *late winter, when the muddy roads are impassable and everyone is stuck at home*
[4] *heaping mockery on me so relentlessly that I felt as if I were standing in front of an archers' target*
[5] *daggers*

At this point Beatrice approaches, and Benedick, unable to face her, makes a hasty exit. Don Pedro regrets the fact that the two of them have fallen out so spectacularly.

Deliberately misinterpreting his words, Beatrice mentions that the two of them were, briefly, romantically attached. That will never happen again, she insists:

Don Pedro: Come, lady, come, you have lost the heart[1] of Signior Benedick.
Beatrice: Indeed, my lord, he lent it me awhile, and I gave him use for it[2] ... Marry, once before he won it of me with false dice;[3] therefore your grace may well say I have lost it.
Don Pedro: You have put him down,[4] lady, you have put him down.
Beatrice: So I would not he should do me,[5] my lord, lest I should prove the mother of fools ...

[1] *friendship, goodwill*
[2] *he gave me his love for a while, and I returned it with interest*
[3] *he won my heart by making false promises*
[4] *crushed him, made a fool of him with your mockery*
[5] *I wouldn't want him to put me down (take me to bed, seduce me)*

Accompanying Beatrice is Count Claudio, who is still dejected after hearing from Don John that he had lost Hero to the prince. However, when Don Pedro reveals the truth, and Leonato confirms it, Claudio is speechless with joy. Beatrice encourages the two lovers to give voice to their feelings:

Don Pedro: ... Claudio, I have wooed in thy name, and fair Hero is won. I have broke[1] with her father, and his good will obtained. Name the day of marriage, and God give thee joy!

Leonato: Count, take of me my daughter, and with her my fortunes. His grace[2] hath made the match, and all grace say amen to it.[3]

Beatrice: Speak, Count, 'tis your cue.

Claudio: Silence is the perfectest herald of joy; I were but little happy if I could say how much.[4] Lady, as you are mine, I am yours ...

Beatrice: Speak, cousin,[5] or, if you cannot, stop his mouth with a kiss and let not him speak neither.

[1] *broached the subject*
[2] *the prince, Don Pedro*
[3] *heaven itself blesses the union*
[4] *my happiness would be limited if I could express it in words*
[5] *Hero*

A wedding is clearly imminent. Beatrice remarks cheerfully that marriage seems to be the eventual fate of everyone except herself. She apologises to the prince for her flippant comments, but he urges her never to change:

Beatrice: ... I beseech your grace pardon me, I was born to speak all mirth and no matter.[1]

Don Pedro: Your silence most offends me,[2] and to be merry best becomes you, for out o'question, you were born in a merry hour.

Beatrice: No, sure, my lord, my mother cried; but then there was a star danced, and under that was I born.

[1] *sense, substance*
[2] *I would prefer you to talk than to be silent*

> *"Hero, only child to Leonato, is his immediate heir, with considerable prospects in land and goods. Her marriage to Claudio is, therefore, a matter for public, as well as private negotiation. It is both a commercial contract and an alliance of families. The match is effected by the powerful and influential Don Pedro on behalf of his protégé, the young Count; backed by such a princely figure, the suitor is accepted before ever Hero has more than a passing acquaintance of her proposed husband ... Hero's own lack of a say in the matter is taken for granted."*
>
> Lisa Jardine, programme notes for the Royal Shakespeare Company production of *Much Ado About Nothing*, 1990

Marriage in mind

When Beatrice has left, Don Pedro remarks on her high spirits. It occurs to him that, despite her protestations, she would make the ideal partner for Benedick. Leonato disagrees:

Don Pedro: She cannot endure to hear tell of a husband.
Leonato: O, by no means. She mocks all her wooers out of suit.[1]
Don Pedro: She were[2] an excellent wife for Benedick.
Leonato: O Lord, my lord, if they were but a week married, they would talk themselves mad.

> [1] *she teases her admirers so relentlessly that they give up*
> [2] *would be*

Don Pedro asks Claudio when he intends to marry. The young man hopes that the ceremony can take place the next day, but Leonato insists that a week is the shortest possible time he needs in order to make all the arrangements.

Claudio is disappointed by the delay. Don Pedro consoles him, explaining that he has a plan which will make the time pass pleasantly:

> *Don Pedro:* ... I warrant[1] thee, Claudio, the time shall not go dully by us. I will, in the interim, undertake one of Hercules' labours, which is, to bring Signior Benedick and the Lady Beatrice into a mountain of affection th'one with th'other.
>
> [1] *guarantee, promise*

Leonato and Claudio are keen to help Don Pedro in his quest to make the couple fall in love. Even Hero agrees, cautiously, to do what she can to bring the two together. The prince assures her that Benedick will prove an excellent match for her cousin:

> *Hero:* I will do any modest office,[1] my lord, to help my cousin to a good husband.
>
> *Don Pedro:* And Benedick is not the unhopefullest husband that I know. Thus far can I praise him: he is of a noble strain, of approved[2] valour and confirmed honesty.[3] I will teach you how to humour[4] your cousin that she shall fall in love with Benedick ...
>
> [1] *carry out any respectable task*
> [2] *proven*
> [3] *honour, integrity*
> [4] *influence*

"The battle between Beatrice and Benedick seems to me to be less a battle between the sexes than a painful, and very funny, mutual baptism. They have in common a refusal to take the plunge ... there is in both an underlying unhappiness with the corner they've painted themselves into."

Director Nicholas Hytner on his 2007 production of *Much Ado About Nothing* at the National Theatre

While Hero is attempting to win over Beatrice, Leonato and Claudio will do the same for Benedick. If they succeed, the prince declares in grandiose terms, it will be a splendid achievement:

> *Don Pedro:* I, with your two helps, will so practise on[1] Benedick
> that, in despite of his quick wit and his queasy
> stomach,[2] he shall fall in love with Beatrice. If we can
> do this, Cupid is no longer an archer; his glory shall be
> ours, for we are the only love-gods.[3]
>
> [1] *work on, manipulate*
> [2] *his perceptiveness and his misgivings about love*
> [3] *Cupid will lose his status as the god of love*

An elaborate deception II, ii

The prince's brother Don John is dismayed to hear that, despite his earlier attempt to deceive Claudio, the count's engagement to Hero is to go ahead. When his companion Borachio mentions that he may be able to frustrate the young couple's wedding plans, Don John demands to know more. His resentment of Claudio continues to eat away at him:

> *Don John:* It is so; the Count Claudio shall marry the daughter
> of Leonato.
> *Borachio:* Yea, my lord, but I can cross[1] it.
> *Don John:* Any bar, any cross, any impediment will be
> medicinable[2] to me. I am sick in displeasure to him,
> and whatsoever comes athwart his affection ranges
> evenly with mine.[3]
>
> [1] *obstruct, disrupt*
> [2] *beneficial*
> [3] *anything that prevents him from achieving his desires*
> *will please me*

Borachio explains that he is on friendly terms with Margaret, one of Hero's maidservants. His plan, which will involve Margaret, will ruin Hero's reputation, with devastating consequences. The plan will first require Don John to tell his brother that Hero, despite her apparent modesty and virtue, is in fact utterly debauched and disloyal.

Irrefutable evidence will be provided to back up this shocking claim, promises Borachio:

> *Borachio:* Go you to the prince your brother; spare not[1] to tell him that he hath wronged his honour in marrying the renowned Claudio – whose estimation do you mightily hold up[2] – to a contaminated stale,[3] such a one as Hero.
>
> *Don John:* What proof shall I make of that?
>
> *Borachio:* Proof enough to misuse[4] the prince, to vex Claudio, to undo Hero, and kill Leonato.
>
> [1] *don't hold back*
> [2] *whose reputation you must resolutely support*
> [3] *prostitute*
> [4] *deceive*

Borachio goes on to describe his scheme. When Don John breaks the news of Hero's depravity to Don Pedro and Claudio, he is to mention Borachio, naming him as Hero's secret lover. Naturally, the two men will demand proof, and on the night before the wedding, Don John will take them to a spot near Hero's bedroom window. There they will see and hear Hero conversing lovingly with Borachio, and they will realise, to their horror, that Don John has been telling the truth.

The woman at the window, of course, will in fact be Margaret; Borachio will persuade her to pretend to be Hero and wear her mistress's nightclothes. Borachio will ensure that Hero herself is absent that night. Don John resolves to put the plan into action. If it succeeds, he will reward Borachio handsomely:

> *Borachio:* … there shall appear such seeming truth of Hero's disloyalty that jealousy shall be called assurance,[1] and all the preparation overthrown.[2]
>
> *Don John:* Grow this to what adverse issue it can,[3] I will put it in practice. Be cunning in the working this and thy fee is a thousand ducats.[4]
>
> [1] *the evidence will be so convincing that their initial doubt will change into certainty*
> [2] *their wedding plans will be ruined*
> [3] *no matter how harmful the outcome may be*
> [4] *gold coins*

The perfect woman

In Leonato's garden, Benedick is alone, musing on the change that seems to have come over his friend Claudio. Since falling in love with Hero, he has lost interest in the rugged simplicity of military life and surrendered to the pleasures of the world:

Benedick: I have known when there was no music with him but the drum and the fife,[1] and now had he rather hear the tabor and the pipe.[2] I have known when he would have walked ten mile afoot to see a good armour, and now he will lie ten nights awake carving the fashion of a new doublet.[3] He was wont to speak plain and to the purpose, like an honest man and a soldier, and now he is turned orthography;[4] his words are a very fantastical banquet ...

[1] *drum and high-pitched flute, used by military bands*
[2] *combination of simple drum and whistle, often played by an individual to accompany dancing and festivities*
[3] *thinking about the design of a sumptuous new jacket*
[4] *adopted a polished, elaborate style of speech*

What kind of man is Benedick? The actor John Gielgud, who played the role in his own successful and long-running production in the 1950s, recalled that his interpretation of the character evolved over time:

"I kept trying to make Benedick into more of a soldier. At first the designer encouraged me to be a dandy, wearing comic hats which used to get laughs the moment I came on in them ... I gradually discarded them, and wore leather doublets and thigh boots and became less of a courtier. I tried to inject a good deal more bluffness and strength into the part. Benedick ought to be an uncouth soldier, a tough misanthrope, who wears a beard and probably smells to high heaven."

John Gielgud, *An Actor and his Time*, 1997

Benedick wonders whether the same might happen to him, but concludes that it is unlikely. His standards are very high, and although he appreciates good qualities in women he is sure he will never find one who possesses them all:

Benedick: One woman is fair, yet I am well.[1] Another is wise, yet I am well. Another virtuous, yet I am well. But till all graces be in one woman, one woman shall not come in my grace.[2]

[1] *unaffected, not tempted*
[2] *gain my favour*

In his mind, Benedick has created a picture of the ideal wife. His demands are exacting, and there is very little scope for variation:

Benedick: Rich she shall be, that's certain; wise, or I'll none;[1] virtuous, or I'll never cheapen[2] her; fair, or I'll never look on her; mild, or come not near me ... Of good discourse,[3] an excellent musician, and her hair shall be – of what colour it please God.

[1] *I'll have nothing to do with her*
[2] *bargain for, make a bid for*
[3] *intelligent conversation*

A musical interlude

Don Pedro now comes out of the house and into the garden. With him are Claudio and Leonato, as well as the prince's attendant Balthasar. Not in the mood for company, Benedick hides in a leafy corner.

Balthasar is an accomplished musician and singer who has been entertaining the gathering. Don Pedro asks to hear one of his favourite songs again. Balthasar's modest reply, the prince believes, is a sign of his genuine talent:

Don Pedro: Come, Balthasar, we'll hear that song again.
Balthasar: O good my lord, tax not so bad a voice
To slander music any more than once.[1]

Don Pedro: It is the witness still of excellency
To put a strange face on his own perfection.[2]
I pray thee sing …

[1] *don't ask me to insult music yet again with my terrible voice*
[2] *it is always a mark of excellence when an artist is critical of his own skill*

Despite Balthasar's protestations, Don Pedro insists on hearing the song, and the two men engage in some courtly word-play:

Don Pedro: … if thou wilt hold longer argument,
Do it in notes.[1]
Balthasar: Note this before my notes:[2]
There's not a note of mine that's worth the noting.[3]
Don Pedro: Why, these are very crotchets[4] that he speaks!

[1] *if you're determined to carry on arguing, do it musically*
[2] *bear this in mind before I start singing*
[3] *it's not worth paying attention to a single note that I sing*
[4] *oddities, nonsense*

Balthasar starts playing his lute. Benedick, from his hiding place, is unimpressed by the player's heartfelt performance. His preference is for the more robust music of the hunting ground:

Benedick: Now is his soul ravished! Is it not strange that sheep's guts[1] should hale[2] souls out of men's bodies? Well, a horn[3] for my money, when all's done.

[1] *the strings of a lute*
[2] *haul, drag*
[3] *hunting-horn*

Balthasar's song is a warning to women about the fickleness of men. Avoid romantic entanglements, the singer advises, and put your energies instead into your own happiness:

> Sigh no more, ladies, sigh no more,
>   Men were deceivers ever; [1]
> One foot in sea, and one on shore,
>   To one thing constant never.
> Then sigh not so, but let them go,
>   And be you blithe and bonny, [2]
> Converting all your sounds of woe
>   Into 'Hey, nonny, nonny'. [3]

[1] always
[2] cheerful, healthy and good-looking
[3] turning your sad groaning into carefree songs

The combative relationship between Beatrice and Benedick seems to have made a strong and lasting impression on the popular imagination. More than twenty years after the play's first performances, the pair are mentioned in a major philosophical work to illustrate a particular type of relationship. The author suggests that the outlook for such couples is hopeful:

"Many times those which at the first sight cannot fancy or affect each other,[1] but are harsh and ready to disagree, offended with each other's carriage,[2] like Benedict and Betteris in the comedy, and in whom they find many faults, by this living together in a house, with conference, kissing, colling[3] and such like allurements, begin, at last, to dote insensibly[4] one upon another."

[1] cannot feel attraction or affection
[2] behaviour
[3] cuddling
[4] devotedly, hopelessly

Robert Burton, *The Anatomy of Melancholy*, 1621

Don Pedro enjoys the song and, as Balthasar leaves, reminds him that he will be singing a serenade outside Hero's window the next night.

A convincing performance

Despite Benedick's attempt to hide, the visitors to the garden are well aware of his presence. Making sure that he can hear them, Don Pedro, Claudio and Leonato now hold a carefully rehearsed conversation. They succeed in giving their friend a shock, as intended:

Don Pedro: Come hither, Leonato. What was it you told me of today? That your niece Beatrice was in love with Signior Benedick?

Claudio: [*aside*] O ay, stalk on, stalk on, the fowl sits.[1] [*aloud*] I did never think that lady would have loved any man.

Leonato: No, nor I neither. But most wonderful[2] that she should so dote on Signior Benedick, whom she hath in all outward behaviours seemed ever to abhor.[3]

Benedick: Is't possible? Sits the wind in that corner?[4]

[1] *carry on with the hunt: our prey is ready to be caught*
[2] *astonishing, extraordinary*
[3] *judging from what she says and does, she has always seemed to detest him*
[4] *is that how things really are?*

The three men continue to express their amazement that Beatrice, of all people, has fallen so passionately in love. They must be telling the truth, concludes Benedick; the news came from the grey-haired, respectable Leonato, who had heard it from his daughter Hero.

Beatrice is tormented by her love, reports Leonato; aware that she has teased Benedick mercilessly in the past, she feels she cannot now admit to him that she loves him. She has attempted many times to put her feelings in a letter, but has never been able to bring herself to send it.

According to Hero, Beatrice curses herself for her past cruelty to Benedick. At this point the description builds up to a melodramatic climax, with the suggestion that Beatrice's sanity, and even her life, may be in danger:

Claudio: … down upon her knees she falls, weeps, sobs, beats her heart, tears her hair, prays, curses: 'O sweet Benedick! God give me patience!'

Leonato: She doth indeed; my daughter says so. And the ecstasy hath so much overborne her [1] that my daughter is sometime afeard she will do a desperate outrage [2] to herself.

[1] *she has been so overwhelmed with passion*
[2] *commit a reckless act of violence*

Making sure that Benedick is still within earshot, Don Pedro and his companions discuss whether their friend should be told of his secret admirer. They take the opportunity to praise Beatrice and mock Benedick at the same time:

Don Pedro: It were good that Benedick knew of it by some other, if she will not discover it. [1]

Claudio: To what end? [2] He would make but a sport of it and torment the poor lady worse.

Don Pedro: An he should, it were an alms to hang him. [3] She's an excellent sweet lady, and, out of all suspicion, she is virtuous.

Claudio: And she is exceeding wise.

Don Pedro: In everything but loving Benedick.

[1] *it would be good if someone could let Benedick know about this, if Beatrice will not reveal her feelings*
[2] *what would that achieve?*
[3] *if he responded like that, hanging would be too good for him*

They agree that Beatrice is caught in a dreadful dilemma, but eventually decide that they should not yet reveal the truth to Benedick. As they leave for dinner, the prince cannot resist a parting shot:

> *Don Pedro:* … we will hear further of it by your daughter.[1] Let it cool the while. I love Benedick well, and I could wish he would modestly examine himself to see how much he is unworthy so good a lady.
>
> [1] *we will discuss the matter further with Hero*

The three companions then go indoors, convinced that their scheme has been successful. All that remains now is for Hero and her attendants to stage a similar conversation while Beatrice is within earshot; events can then be left to take their course, and love will surely blossom between the two adversaries.

A changed man

Alone again, Benedick emerges from the foliage. The conversation that he has just overheard has affected him profoundly. His true feelings for Beatrice have suddenly become clear to him, and his friends' critical comments, far from wounding him, have made him determined to change his attitude:

> *Benedick:* It seems her affections have their full bent.[1] Love me? Why, it must be requited[2] … I did never think to marry. I must not seem proud; happy are they that hear their detractions and can put them to mending.[3]
>
> [1] *her feelings are stretched to the limit; she is utterly in love*
> [2] *given in return*
> [3] *hear their faults criticised and respond positively*

The prince's admiring remarks about Beatrice are completely justified, realises Benedick. He is determined to prove that, in falling in love with him, she has made the right choice. He will be wholehearted and tenacious in his love for her:

Benedick: They say the lady is fair – 'tis a truth, I can bear them witness. And virtuous – 'tis so, I cannot reprove[1] it. And wise, but[2] for loving me. By my troth, it is no addition to her wit – nor no great argument of her folly,[3] for I will be horribly in love with her.

[1] *refute, contradict*
[2] *except*
[3] *loving me may not be a sign of wisdom, but I will make sure it is not evidence of foolishness either*

His friends will mock him, no doubt, at his sudden change of heart; after all, he has often held forth about his distaste for love and marriage. The prospect does not bother him. People change, reasons Benedick, and his own role in the world is about to be transformed. He brushes aside the concern that his past words will be used against him:

Benedick: … doth not the appetite alter? A man loves the meat in his youth that he cannot endure in his age. Shall quips and sentences[1] and these paper bullets of the brain[2] awe a man from the career of his humour?[3] No, the world must be peopled.[4] When I said I would die a bachelor, I did not think I should live till I were married.

[1] *trite observations, clichés*
[2] *words which, though meant to wound, are feeble and harmless*
[3] *deter a man from pursuing his desires*
[4] *populated*

At this point Beatrice herself comes into the garden. She is in an irritable frame of mind, having been sent reluctantly to summon Benedick for dinner. Benedick, however, is sure that he can detect signs of the passionate love that she has been keeping to herself:

Benedick:	Here comes Beatrice. By this day, she's a fair lady! I do spy some marks of love in her.
Beatrice:	Against my will I am sent to bid you come in to dinner.
Benedick:	Fair Beatrice, I thank you for your pains.[1]
Beatrice:	I took no more pains for those thanks than you take pains to thank me.[2] If it had been painful I would not have come.

[1] *taking the trouble, making an effort*
[2] *it was just as easy for me to pass on the message as it is for you to thank me*

Unwilling to stop and talk, Beatrice hastily goes back indoors. Convinced that she is hiding her affection behind her abrupt manner, Benedick follows her adoringly into the house.

"The longer you ponder Beatrice, the more enigmatic she becomes ... The fascination of Beatrice is founded upon her extraordinary blend of merriment and bitterness."

Harold Bloom, *Shakespeare: The Invention of the Human*, 1998

Another eavesdropper

Later, Hero is in the garden with her attendants Margaret and Ursula: the next part of Don Pedro's plan is about to take place. Hero sends Margaret indoors to tell Beatrice that her friends outside are talking about her. Margaret is to suggest that Beatrice hides herself in a suitably sheltered spot, from which she can listen to the conversation in secrecy.

Margaret hurries into the house. Hero reminds Ursula what their subject-matter is to be as they pass Beatrice's hiding place:

Hero:	… Our talk must only be of Benedick.
	When I do name him, let it be thy part
	To praise him more than ever man did merit;
	My talk to thee must be how Benedick
	Is sick in love with Beatrice. Of this matter
	Is little Cupid's crafty arrow made …

As expected, Beatrice now comes out into the garden, keen to hear what is being said about her, and hides in the leafy alcove suggested by Margaret. As Hero and Ursula walk past, they pretend to be in mid-conversation. Hero assures her companion that her news about Benedick comes from his two closest friends, Don Pedro and Claudio:

Hero:	[*to Ursula*]
	Then go we near her, that her ear lose nothing [1]
	Of the false sweet bait that we lay for it.
	[*they approach Beatrice's hiding place*]
	– No, truly, Ursula, she is too disdainful.
	I know her spirits are as coy [2] and wild
	As haggards of the rock. [3]
Ursula:	But are you sure
	That Benedick loves Beatrice so entirely?
Hero:	So says the prince and my new-trothed lord.

[1] *so that she doesn't miss a word*
[2] *haughty, aloof*
[3] *fierce, untrained hawks*

Hero has decided not to tell Beatrice of Benedick's love; it would be better for him to suppress his feelings, she claims, and remain silent on the matter. When questioned by Ursula, she explains that Beatrice's proud nature makes it impossible for her to love another person fully:

Hero: I know he doth deserve
               As much as may be yielded to a man.[1]
               But Nature never framed a woman's heart
               Of prouder stuff than that of Beatrice.
               Disdain and scorn ride sparkling in her eyes,
               Misprising[2] what they look on, and her wit
               Values itself so highly that to her
               All matter else seems weak.[3]

               [1] *as much praise as may be given to any man*
               [2] *undervaluing, scorning*
               [3] *all other subjects seem of little worth*

Ursula agrees; if Beatrice finds out that Benedick loves her, she will only make fun of him. Warming to her theme, Hero accuses her cousin of deliberately seeing the worst in all her potential admirers. Any quality that might be considered a virtue is seen instead as a fault:

Hero: … If speaking, why, a vane blown with all winds; [1]
               If silent, why, a block moved with none.[2]
               So turns she every man the wrong side out,
               And never gives to truth and virtue that
               Which simpleness and merit purchaseth.[3]

               [1] *if a man is talkative, she will describe him as a*
                   windbag who has an opinion on everything
               [2] *if he is quiet, she will call him unfeeling and*
                   slow-witted
               [3] *never recognises simple integrity and merit for*
                   the good qualities that they are

Hero cannot criticise Beatrice to her face, she claims, as she would face a withering onslaught of mockery. The same would happen to Benedick if he were to express his feelings for her, so it is safer if he keeps the truth to himself, even though the consequences may be terrible:

Hero: If I should speak,
She would mock me into air. O, she would laugh me
Out of myself, press me to death with wit! [1]
Therefore let Benedick, like covered fire,
Consume away in sighs, waste inwardly. [2]
It were [3] a better death than die with mocks ...

[1] *she would ridicule me into oblivion, reduce me to silence, and suffocate me with her humour*
[2] *slowly waste away, like an enclosed, tightly-packed fire*
[3] *would be*

Benedick must be dissuaded from loving Beatrice, declares Hero. Ursula is dubious; surely, with her renowned astuteness, Beatrice can see that Benedick would be the perfect husband. He has a well deserved reputation, she points out, for his good looks, bravery and intelligence.

Believing that their conversation has had the desired effect, the two women now change the subject, and discuss Hero's marriage. The ceremony takes place tomorrow, Hero confirms, and she asks Ursula to come into the house to help choose a wedding dress. As they leave the garden, they comment excitedly on the success of their scheme:

Ursula: [*to Hero*] She's limed,[1] I warrant you! We have caught her, madam!
Hero: [*to Ursula*] If it prove so, then loving goes by haps; [2]
Some Cupid kills with arrows, some with traps.

[1] *ensnared, like a bird in a trap*
[2] *falling in love involves an element of chance*

Beatrice now emerges from her hiding place into the garden. Like Benedick before her, she has been profoundly affected by the overheard conversation. She realises that she loves Benedick, and resolves to shed her brash exterior and declare her true feelings:

Beatrice: What fire is in mine ears? Can this be true?
            Stand I condemned for pride and scorn so much?
            Contempt, farewell; and maiden pride, adieu;
            No glory lives behind the back of such.[1]
            And Benedick, love on, I will requite thee[2] ...

[1] *people with these qualities will never flourish*
[2] *return your love*

> *"The love between Benedick and Beatrice in* Much Ado *is the effect of elaborately fictitious information fed to each partner, so that it is impossible to decide whether this groundless discourse uncovers a love which was 'naturally' there, or actually constructs it."*
>
> Terry Eagleton, *William Shakespeare*, 1986

Lovesickness

Back in Leonato's house, the prince tells his friends that he will return to Aragon when Claudio's wedding has taken place. Claudio volunteers to escort him, but Don Pedro dismisses the idea; Claudio must remain with his new wife. Instead, he suggests that Benedick should accompany him.

It immediately becomes clear that Benedick has undergone a radical change of some kind: he has had a shave and smartened his clothes, and his manner seems more serious. It cannot be love, Don Pedro declares, as Benedick has repeatedly denounced it as a foolish indulgence; if he seems preoccupied, he must be short of money. Benedick claims that there is a simple reason for his pensive mood:

Benedick:	Gallants, I am not as I have been.
Leonato:	So say I; methinks you are sadder.[1]
Claudio:	I hope he be in love.
Don Pedro:	Hang him, truant![2] There's no true drop of blood[3] in him to be truly touched with love. If he be sad, he wants[4] money.
Benedick:	I have the toothache.

[1] *more earnest and thoughtful*
[2] *if that were true, he should be hanged as a traitor*
[3] *not a trace of passion*
[4] *lacks, needs*

The mockery continues as Benedick's companions comment on his appearance, his mood, and his clothes: he is even wearing perfume, they claim, another sure sign of a man in love. They hint playfully that they know the identity of the lady in question.

Benedick, vexed by his friends' relentless teasing, tells Leonato that he wants a word in private, and the two men leave. Claudio and Don Pedro are delighted: Benedick is clearly going to approach Leonato about marrying his niece, Beatrice.

A chill descends

At this point the prince's brother Don John enters. The light-hearted mood changes suddenly as he implies that Claudio's wedding may not go ahead as planned:

Don John: [*to Claudio*] Means your lordship to be married
          tomorrow?
Don Pedro: You know he does.
Don John: I know not that[1] when he knows what I know.

> [1] *that may not be the case; I'm not sure of that*

Don John assures Claudio that, even though he is bringing unpleasant news, he has the young man's interests at heart. Don Pedro's efforts in bringing Hero and Claudio together were sadly misguided, he says. The two men become impatient, and Don John comes straight to the point, leaving his listeners stunned. Not only is Hero unfaithful to Claudio, her promiscuity is the subject of public gossip:

Don John: I came hither to tell you; and, circumstances shortened[1]
          – for she has been too long a-talking of[2] – the lady is
          disloyal.
Claudio: Who, Hero?
Don John: Even she: Leonato's Hero, your Hero, every man's Hero.
Claudio: Disloyal?
Don John: The word is too good to paint out[3] her wickedness; I
          could say she were worse.

> [1] *to put it briefly*
> [2] *people have been talking about her for too long*
> [3] *fully describe*

"Hero says far less than the other major characters, but we hear her name more often than that of any other character. And when we begin to look at her in this light we come to the centre of the play, for talking about people is the play's central activity."

Jonathan Bate, Introduction to the RSC Shakespeare
edition of *Much Ado About Nothing*, 2009

This very evening, promises Don John, he will take the two men to a spot from where they will be able to observe Hero receiving a night-time visitor. Claudio and Don Pedro, in their state of shock, are unwilling to believe what they have heard. Don John insists, again, that they will see the evidence of Hero's infidelity with their own eyes.

The two men's shock quickly turns to anger at Hero and her dishonesty. If this report is true, they vow, tomorrow they will denounce her publicly, in the church where she was due to be married. Don John urges them to remain calm until they have seen proof of Hero's debauchery. In the end they will be glad, he promises, that this disastrous marriage has been averted:

Don John:	Bear it coldly[1] but till midnight, and let the issue show itself.[2]
Don Pedro:	O day untowardly turned![3]
Claudio:	O mischief strangely thwarting![4]
Don John:	O plague right well prevented! So you will say when you have seen the sequel.[5]

[1] *calmly*
[2] *let events unfold*
[3] *unhappily changed*
[4] *evil that has unexpectedly ruined our plans*
[5] *what will happen tonight*

> *"As the plot unravels, it becomes more and more clear that the social and verbal graces enacted at the court are a thin and self-conscious performance. Claudio's seemingly honourable character, and his stiff proposals of love, seem insincere and empty when we see how willingly he and the prince will take on their brutal role in publicly shaming Hero."*
>
> Andrea Varney, *Deception and Dramatic Irony in* Much Ado About Nothing, 2016

Keeping the peace

Late at night, on the streets of Messina, the chief constable Dogberry and his assistant Verges are organising the watch, a band of citizens responsible for patrolling the streets and keeping the city safe.

Dogberry's first task is to select a citizen to lead the watch. It quickly becomes clear that he and Verges, despite their rank, are confused and slow-witted, with a poor grasp of language and an even poorer grasp of the duties of the watch. Having selected an individual on the basis that he can read and write, Dogberry hands him a lantern and instructs him and his companions on their responsibilities. Their main aim, apparently, is to avoid confrontation:

Dogberry:	[*to the leading watchman*] You are thought here to be the most senseless[1] and fit man for the constable of the watch,[2] therefore bear you the lantern. This is your charge: you shall comprehend all vagrom men.[3] You are to bid any man stand,[4] in the prince's name.
Watchman:	How if 'a[5] will not stand?
Dogberry:	Why then, take no note of him, but let him go, and presently call the rest of the watch together, and thank God you are rid of a knave.

[1] *sensible*
[2] *leader of the watch; Dogberry's deputy*
[3] *arrest all vagrants*
[4] *stop for questioning*
[5] *he*

The watch is to go about the city quietly, Dogberry tells them. The watchmen take the command to its logical extreme, but Dogberry is satisfied:

> *Dogberry:* You shall also make no noise in the streets: for, for the watch to babble and to talk is most tolerable,[1] and not to be endured.
>
> *Watchman:* We will rather sleep than talk; we know what belongs to a watch.[2]
>
> *Dogberry:* Why, you speak like an ancient[3] and most quiet watchman, for I cannot see how sleeping should offend. Only have a care that your bills[4] be not stolen.

[1] *intolerable*
[2] *how a watch should behave*
[3] *experienced*
[4] *weapons; long wooden axes tipped with spikes*

The names of the principal characters of *Much Ado About Nothing* – such as Don Pedro, Claudio and Leonato – generally reflect their origins in various Spanish and Italian cities. Shakespeare's two constables of the Watch, by contrast, are more reminiscent of provincial England:

"*Much Ado About Nothing is set almost entirely in a house in a golden Mediterranean town enjoying victory celebrations. The house is warmly, even lovingly, described. At the Governor's, life is comfortable, gracious, and witty ... Verbal sport of a less knowing kind comes from Dogberry, Verges, and the Watch, who wander in as it might be from Sheep Street, Stratford-upon-Avon. Theirs is an English kind of bumbling ...*"

David Daniell, *Shakespeare and the Traditions of Comedy*, 1986

Drunks are to be asked to leave the alehouses and go home to bed, Dogberry advises. If they refuse, they should be left alone until they are sober, and then given a mild reprimand. Thieves may be treated even more leniently. If possible, they should be avoided completely:

Dogberry: If you meet a thief, you may suspect him, by virtue of your office, to be no true[1] man. And for such kind of men, the less you meddle or make with[2] them, why, the more is for your honesty.

[1] *honest*
[2] *get involved with, have to do with*

Any thieves that the watch happens to come across should preferably be allowed to slip away unnoticed, suggests Dogberry, pleased with his own witticism:

Watchman: If we know him to be a thief, shall we not lay hands on him?
Dogberry: Truly, by your office you may;[1] but I think they that touch pitch[2] will be defiled. The most peaceable way for you, if you do take a thief, is to let him show himself what he is,[3] and steal out of your company.

[1] *you have the authority to do so*
[2] *sticky, tar-like substance*
[3] *demonstrate his true nature*

Dogberry and Verges now leave, and the watchmen settle down on a nearby bench. Dogberry suddenly remembers an important event that is soon to take place, and he gives the men a final piece of advice:

Dogberry: I pray you watch about Signior Leonato's door, for the wedding being there tomorrow, there is a great coil[1] tonight.

[1] *commotion, hubbub*

Under arrest

A sudden noise in the street catches the watchmen's attention. Don John's attendant Borachio is calling out drunkenly to his friend Conrade. He has carried out an important task on behalf of his corrupt master, and is celebrating a financial windfall:

Borachio: … I have earned of Don John a thousand ducats.
Conrade: Is it possible that any villainy should be so dear?
Borachio: Thou shouldst rather ask if it were possible any villainy should be so rich. For when rich villains have need of poor ones, poor ones may make what price they will.[1]

> [1] *poor villains like me can demand as much money as they want*

Earlier in the night, as planned, Borachio climbed up to Hero's bedroom window. Margaret, dressed in Hero's nightclothes, was ready and waiting:

Borachio: … I have tonight wooed Margaret, the Lady Hero's gentlewoman, by the name of Hero; she leans me out[1] at her mistress' chamber window, bids me a thousand times goodnight …

> [1] *leans out for me*

Don John had taken his brother and Claudio to a corner of the garden to observe the encounter. The ruse was a complete success, declares Borachio proudly. Don Pedro and Claudio are now convinced that Hero has a secret lover, and intend to shame her in public at tomorrow's wedding:

Conrade: And thought they Margaret was Hero?
Borachio: Two of them did, the prince and Claudio, but the devil my master knew she was Margaret. And partly by his oaths, which first possessed them,[1] partly by the dark night, which did deceive them, but chiefly by my villainy, which did confirm any slander that Don John had made, away went Claudio enraged, swore he would

meet her as he was appointed next morning at the temple,[2] and there, before the whole congregation, shame her with what he saw o'ernight ...

[1] *by Don John's sworn allegations, which first persuaded them*
[2] *church*

The watch, meanwhile, are unsure what to make of the overheard conversation. Despite their confusion, however, they decide that something shady is going on, and that their superiors must be informed. Weapons at the ready, they arrest the pair without further ado:

1st Watchman: We charge you in the prince's name, stand!
2nd Watchman: Call up the right master constable![1] We have here recovered[2] the most dangerous piece of lechery[3] that ever was known in the commonwealth!

[1] *the chief constable, Dogberry*
[2] *discovered*
[3] *treachery*

We have here recovered the most dangerous piece of lechery ...

It is the incompetent, misguided watchmen who first stumble across the plot against Hero:

"It is part of the irony which underlies the play, that in this community of brilliantly accomplished men and women, it is not by dint of wit but through the blind channels of accident and unreason that the discovery makes its way."

Israel Gollancz, Introduction to *Much Ado About Nothing*, 1909

Another casualty

Hero's wedding-day has arrived. It is early morning, and, with the help of her attendants Margaret and Ursula, she is busy making last-minute preparations. She sends Ursula off to fetch Beatrice, and agitatedly discusses details of her clothes and appearance with Margaret.

They talk about her wedding dress, and Hero remarks that she is anxious about the coming day. She scolds Margaret for her bawdy comment:

Hero:	God give me joy to wear it, for my heart is exceeding heavy.
Margaret:	'Twill be heavier soon by the weight of a man.
Hero:	Fie upon thee! Art not ashamed?

Margaret, who is in a particularly talkative mood, defends herself vigorously: marriage is an honourable institution, and should be celebrated unashamedly.

At this point Beatrice arrives. Like Benedick, she has been affected deeply by overhearing talk of her secret admirer; and like him she claims to be unwell. The others tease her, realising that she not ill but lovesick. To Hero's amusement, Margaret hands Beatrice a remedy that happens to suggest the name of her beloved:

Beatrice:	By my troth, I am sick.
Margaret:	Get you some of this distilled *carduus benedictus*,[1] and lay it to your heart; it is the only thing for a qualm.[2]
Hero:	There thou prick'st[3] her with a thistle.
Beatrice:	*Benedictus*? Why *benedictus*? You have some moral[4] in this *benedictus*.

[1] *type of thistle believed to have healing properties*
[2] *sudden feeling of faintness or sickness*
[3] *provoke, arouse*
[4] *hidden meaning*

Margaret strenuously denies that she is thinking of anyone in particular. In the midst of her effusive reply, however, she cannot help mentioning that Benedick has changed his mind when it comes to love and marriage:

Margaret: Moral? No, by my troth, I have no moral meaning ...
               I cannot think, if I would think my heart out of thinking,
               that you are in love, or that you will be in love, or that
               you can be in love. Yet Benedick was such another,[1]
               and now is he become a man.[2]

               [1] *another person who, like you, rejected the idea of love*
               [2] *susceptible to love, like any other man*

Ursula now hurries in. The bridegroom is on his way, she reports, accompanied by all his friends: it is time to go to church.

A message for the governor   III, v

Constables Dogberry and Verges have been told by the watch that two suspicious characters, found wandering around the streets late last night, have been arrested. The constables have come to inform the governor, Leonato, of the situation.

Their constant digressions, interruptions and misunderstandings make it difficult for Leonato to establish what the officers of the law are trying to tell him. He is about to attend his daughter's wedding, and time is short:

Leonato: Brief, I pray you, for you see it is a busy time with me.
Dogberry: Marry, this it is, sir.
Verges: Yes, in truth it is, sir.
Leonato: What is it, my good friends?
Dogberry: Goodman Verges, sir, speaks a little off the matter.[1] An
             old man, sir, and his wits are not so blunt[2] as, God help,
             I would desire they were; but, in faith, honest as the
             skin between his brows.
Verges: Yes, I thank God, I am as honest as any man living, that
             is an old man and no honester than I.

             [1] *is rambling, is missing the point*
             [2] *sharp*

Rather than convey their news, Dogberry is keen to explain that his assistant is becoming talkative and confused in his old age. Leonato manages, with difficulty, to keep his impatience in check:

Leonato: I would fain[1] know what you have to say.

Verges: Marry, sir, our watch tonight, excepting[2] your worship's presence, have ta'en a couple of as arrant[3] knaves as any in Messina.

Dogberry: A good old man, sir, he will be talking. As they say, 'When the age is in, the wit is out.' ... But, God is to be worshipped, all men are not alike.

Leonato: Indeed, neighbour, he comes too short of you.

[1] *gladly*
[2] *respecting*
[3] *outright, notorious*

Leonato insists that he can stay no longer, and Dogberry finally manages to make himself clear: he wants the governor to question the two suspects this morning. With the wedding imminent, Leonato instructs Dogberry to carry out the questioning himself, and hurries off to church.

> *"Dogberry likes to hear himself talk as well as Beatrice and Benedick do, and he, too, is interested in words for their own sake. The parody is apparent ... it sets us wondering how much there is to choose between the repartee of the wits and the mental meanderings of the constable, between the polishing of the King's English by Beatrice and Benedick and the murdering of it by Dogberry."*
>
> Harold C. Goddard, *The Meaning of Shakespeare*, 1951

Hero is accused

Everyone has come to the wedding: as well as the bride and groom, Hero's father Leonato and her cousin Beatrice are there, as are prince Don Pedro and his brother Don John, Claudio's friend Benedick and others.

Leonato urges Friar Francis, who is to conduct the service, to keep it as succinct as possible. On hearing Claudio's unexpected answer to the friar's question, Leonato assumes that there has been a simple misunderstanding:

Friar:	You come hither, my lord, to marry this lady?
Claudio:	No.
Leonato:	To be married to her, Friar; you come to marry her.

The friar asks, in the traditional manner, whether the couple are aware of any reason why the marriage should not take place. When Leonato interjects on Claudio's behalf, the young man's response is impassioned and ominous:

Friar:	If either of you know any inward[1] impediment why you should not be conjoined, I charge you on your souls to utter it.
Claudio:	Know you any, Hero?
Hero:	None, my lord.
Friar:	Know you any, Count?
Leonato:	I dare make his answer: none.
Claudio:	O, what men dare do! What men may do! What men daily do, not knowing what they do!

[1] *secret, hidden*

Claudio interrupts the proceedings and addresses Leonato directly. He asks whether there is anything he can give back to Leonato in return for his daughter. Don Pedro suggests that the only offering of equal value would be Hero herself.

A wave of horror and disbelief sweeps through the church as Claudio, taking his cue from the prince, rejects Hero contemptuously. He urges onlookers not to be swayed by her convincing performance of modesty. In truth, she is little better than a prostitute:

> Claudio: There, Leonato, take her back again.
> Give not this rotten orange[1] to your friend;
> She's but the sign and semblance of her honour.[2]
> Behold how like a maid[3] she blushes here!
> ... Would you not swear,
> All you that see her, that she were a maid,
> By these exterior shows? But she is none;
> She knows the heat of a luxurious[4] bed.
> Her blush is guiltiness, not modesty.

[1] *fruit associated with prostitution*
[2] *she only has the appearance of virtue*
[3] *virgin*
[4] *lustful, debauched*

Perhaps Claudio means that he has already slept with his future wife, suggests Leonato. Claudio contradicts him immediately: he has always behaved with absolute propriety, he insists. When Hero tries to defend herself, he turns on her angrily. Shocked at his inexplicable outburst, Hero is concerned for his well-being:

> Claudio: No, Leonato,
> I never tempted her with word too large,[1]
> But as a brother to his sister showed
> Bashful sincerity and comely love.
> Hero: And seemed I ever otherwise to you?
> Claudio: Out on thee, seeming![2]
> ... you are more intemperate in your blood
> Than Venus, or those pampered animals
> That rage in savage sensuality.[3]
> Hero: Is my lord well that he doth speak so wide?[4]

[1] *lewd, indecent*
[2] *shame on your pretence*
[3] *pets that are indulged and allowed to run wild*
[4] *misguidedly*

In desperation, Leonato turns to Don Pedro. He is appalled to hear the prince repeat Claudio's accusation, expressing his regret that he helped to arrange the marriage. Don John adds his voice to the condemnation:

Leonato: Sweet prince, why speak not you?
Don Pedro: What should I speak?
I stand dishonoured that have gone about [1]
To link my dear friend to a common stale. [2]
Leonato: Are these things spoken, or do I but dream?
Don John: Sir, they are spoken, and these things are true.

[1] *as the person who has arranged*
[2] *prostitute*

Claudio demands to know what happened last night. When Hero denies any wrongdoing, the prince describes the scene that they witnessed with their own eyes. Don John implores his brother not to go into detail, as Hero's immorality is so repugnant:

Claudio: What man was he talked with you yesternight
Out at your window betwixt twelve and one?
Now, if you are a maid, answer to this.
Hero: I talked with no man at that hour, my lord.
Don Pedro: Why, then you are no maiden. Leonato,
I am sorry you must hear. Upon mine honour,
Myself, my brother and this grieved Count
Did see her, hear her, at that hour last night,
Talk with a ruffian at her chamber window,
Who hath indeed, most like a liberal [1] villain,
Confessed the vile encounters they have had
A thousand times in secret.
Don John: Fie, fie, they are not to be named, my lord,
Not to be spoke of!

[1] *uninhibited, shameless*

Claudio will never trust beauty again, he vows; for him, love has lost its charms. Overcome with anguish, Hero falls to the ground, unconscious.

A desperate remedy

Hero's three accusers leave the church. Beatrice rushes to the aid of her cousin, fearing that she may be dead. It would be better if she were, declares Leonato, distraught at the scandal that his daughter has caused. Indeed, if she is not dead, he threatens, he will kill her himself. In the past he has lamented the fact that he had only one child, but now he wishes she had never been born:

Leonato: Grieved I, I had but one?[1]
Chid I for that at frugal Nature's frame?[2]
O, one too much by thee! Why had I one?
Why ever wast thou lovely in my eyes?

[1] *did I grieve because I had only one child?*
[2] *did I reproach Nature for her ungenerous plans?*

If he had adopted a child, he reasons, he could ascribe her wickedness to an unknown father, but he cannot disclaim responsibility for Hero's character. Nothing can ever atone for her offence; she is sullied for ever. Benedick urges him to remain calm and withhold judgement, while Beatrice is certain that the accusation is false:

Leonato: ... O, she is fallen
Into a pit of ink that the wide sea
Hath drops too few to wash her clean again,
And salt too little which may season give[1]
To her foul-tainted flesh.
Benedick: Sir, sir, be patient.
For my part, I am so attired in wonder[2]
I know not what to say.
Beatrice: O, on my soul, my cousin is belied![3]

[1] *preserve, cleanse*
[2] *overcome with amazement*
[3] *slandered; the victim of a lie*

> *There, Leonato, take her back again.*
> *Give not this rotten orange to your friend ...*
>
> *"The scene of Claudio and Hero's interrupted wedding shows how the male characters, even her father, line up behind the angry groom, who rejects his bride in terms that confirm that she is a transaction between the play's menfolk ... Only Beatrice is utterly loyal to her cousin."*
>
> Emma Smith, *Comedy, tragedy and gender politics in Much Ado About Nothing*, 2016

Benedick asks Beatrice whether she was with Hero last night. She answers that, although the cousins often slept in the same room, they were not together last night. Leonato takes this as further evidence that Claudio's accusation is true. Besides, he argues, there is no reason for the prince and Claudio to lie about such an important matter.

Hero is starting to recover, and Friar Francis, who has been observing her carefully, now speaks up. It is clear to him that there has been a terrible mistake. Everything about Hero's behaviour, he believes, proclaims her innocence. Leonato remains adamant; after all, Hero has not denied the allegations.

The friar questions her directly, and Hero passionately insists that she knows nothing of the incident that the others claim to have witnessed last night:

Friar:	Lady, what man is he you are accused of?
Hero:	They know that do accuse me.[1] I know none.

                                      ... O my father,
Prove you[2] that any man with me conversed
At hours unmeet,[3] or that I yesternight
Maintained the change of words[4] with any creature,
Refuse me, hate me, torture me to death!

[1] *only my accusers know who they mean*
[2] *if you can prove*
[3] *improper, inappropriate*
[4] *exchanged words, engaged in conversation*

Benedick, like the friar, believes that some dreadful error must lie behind his friends' shocking conduct. His suspicions centre on one man, the prince's illegitimate brother:

Benedick: Two of them have the very bent of honour; [1]
And if their wisdoms be misled in this,
The practice [2] of it lives in John the bastard,
Whose spirits toil in frame of villainies. [3]

> [1] *Don Pedro and Claudio are totally committed to behaving honourably*
> [2] *scheming, carrying out*
> [3] *who devotes himself to malicious plots*

Leonato, still in a volatile, vengeful frame of mind, asserts that he will take Hero's life if she is guilty; but if she is the victim of treachery, he will take swift and bloody revenge on the perpetrators.

To an audience of Shakespeare's time, the public accusation of Hero might have brought to mind the proceedings of a church court. Although these courts dealt with a range of religious and moral issues, the high proportion of cases involving fornication, adultery, and illegitimate births earned them the nickname 'bawdy courts':

"Every time the bawdy court was set up in a parish church, a place of worship was converted into a place of litigation. Such an instant transformation of church into bawdy court occurs in the wedding ceremony scene of Much Ado About Nothing *when Claudio accuses Hero of infidelity. The Friar's role switches from that of minister performing the sacrament of marriage to bawdy court judge hearing a case of sexual slander."*

Jonathan Bate, *Soul of the Age*, 2009

The friar attempts to calm Leonato. He puts forward a plan which, he hopes, might resolve the situation. As far as her accusers know, the friar points out, Hero has died from the shock of their revelations. He suggests that Hero should be kept in seclusion for the time being: meanwhile, her death will be officially announced, and a suitable ceremony will take place.

As a result, believes the friar, her accusers' attitudes will soften. It is human nature to value things more highly once they have been lost, and Claudio's love for Hero will surely be rekindled when he learns of her death:

Friar: ... what we have we prize not to the worth[1]
                Whiles we enjoy it, but being lacked and lost,
                Why, then we rack the value,[2] then we find
                The virtue that possession would not show us
                Whiles it was ours. So will it fare with Claudio:
                When he shall hear she died upon[3] his words,
                Th'idea of her life shall sweetly creep
                Into his study of imagination[4] ...

[1] *do not value at its full worth*
[2] *consider it far more valuable*
[3] *on hearing*
[4] *his imaginative musings*

The friar hopes that Claudio will, eventually, come to regret his harsh treatment of Hero. There may yet be a happy ending, he suggests. Even if people do not react as he expects, at least the report of her death should silence any talk about her supposed infidelity. At worst, Hero can take refuge in a nunnery, where she will be out of harm's way.

Leonato, still overwhelmed with grief and pain, accepts the friar's proposed plan: Hero's death will shortly be announced, and all those now present in the church will confirm that she died on hearing Claudio's denunciation. The friar tries to comfort Hero, and encourages her to remain optimistic:

Friar: Come, lady, die to live. This wedding day
           Perhaps is but prolonged.[1] Have patience and endure.

[1] *postponed*

A lover's vow

The friar leads Hero and her father away, leaving Beatrice and Benedick alone in the church. Beatrice has been in tears at the ill-treatment of her cousin, and Benedick agrees that Hero has been wronged. There is something that can be done to make amends, Beatrice hints; Benedick, keen to ease her distress, wishes to know more. First, however, they talk warily of their feelings for one another:

Benedick: I do love nothing in the world so well as you. Is not that strange?

Beatrice: As strange as the thing I know not.[1] It were[2] as possible for me to say I loved nothing so well as you, but believe me not; and yet I lie not. I confess nothing, nor I deny nothing.

[1] *as strange as anything unknown to me might be*
[2] *would be*

Benedick becomes more insistent. He is sure that Beatrice loves him, and ardently declares his own love. Beatrice remains cautious. Perhaps his vows are insincere:

Benedick: By my sword, Beatrice, thou lovest me.

Beatrice: Do not swear and eat it.[1]

Benedick: I will swear by it[2] that you love me, and I will make him eat it that says I love not you.[3]

Beatrice: Will you not eat your word?

Benedick: With no sauce that can be devised to it. I protest I love thee.

[1] *eat your words, change your mind*
[2] *by my sword*
[3] *I will kill anyone who says that I don't love you*

Beatrice finally reveals that she feels the same way about Benedick. He is keen to prove his love to her, but Beatrice's response comes as a shock:

Beatrice:	… I was about to protest I loved you.
Benedick:	And do it, with all thy heart.
Beatrice:	I love you with so much of my heart that none is left to protest.
Benedick:	Come, bid me do anything for thee.
Beatrice:	Kill Claudio.

Benedick reacts with horror; the very idea of killing his friend is intolerable. Beatrice starts to walk away angrily. Benedick urges her to stay, or at least to leave on friendly terms. Her response is scornful. She would kill Claudio herself if she were a man, she asserts furiously:

Beatrice:	You dare easier be friends with me than fight with mine enemy.
Benedick:	Is Claudio thine enemy?
Beatrice:	Is 'a[1] not approved in the height[2] a villain, that hath slandered, scorned, dishonoured my kinswoman? O, that I were a man! What, bear her in hand until they come to take hands,[3] and then with public accusation, uncovered slander, unmitigated rancour[4] – O God, that I were a man! I would eat his heart in the marketplace.

[1] *he*
[2] *absolutely proved*
[3] *lead her on with false hopes until their marriage*
[4] *blatant lies and sheer spite*

Benedick attempts to calm her down, but Beatrice becomes increasingly enraged as she thinks about the injustice done to her cousin. The story about the man at her bedroom window is clearly nonsense, she cries, and Claudio and the prince have made themselves look ridiculous with their deluded outburst. Like so many men, she remarks scathingly, they are obsessed with courtly behaviour, fine clothes and elegant language.

Benedick eventually asks Beatrice a direct question, and her reply spurs him on to make a momentous decision. Either he or Claudio will die:

Benedick:	Tarry, good Beatrice. By this hand, I love thee.
Beatrice:	Use it for my love some other way than swearing by it.
Benedick:	Think you in your soul the Count Claudio hath wronged Hero?
Beatrice:	Yea, as sure as I have a thought or a soul.
Benedick:	Enough, I am engaged.[1] I will challenge him.[2] I will kiss your hand, and so I leave you. By this hand, Claudio shall render me a dear account.[3]

[1] *committed, pledged*
[2] *challenge him to a duel*
[3] *will pay dearly for his actions*

"The scene of Hero's rejection in church presents a crisis of spiritual values. Beatrice acts on her faith in her cousin, and Benedick acts on his faith in Beatrice. This involvement in a serious issue brings them together utterly, completing the work of their friends' earlier ploys. This process permits them to return to the world of normal relations, where earlier they had isolated themselves from it."

Charles Boyce, *Shakespeare A to Z*, 1990

The truth emerges

The watchmen have taken Borachio and Conrade into custody, where they are to be questioned by the constables, Dogberry and Verges. The sexton, a church official, has been called in to oversee proceedings and make a written record for the attention of the governor.

Dogberry, as ever, is pompous, confused and long-winded. He engages in some meaningless discussion with the accused, ordering the sexton to note every detail. Losing patience, the sexton suggests that he questions the watchmen to hear their accusations.

The watchmen's answers are significant, but Dogberry manages to misinterpret them:

> *Dogberry:* Masters, I charge you in the prince's name, accuse these men.
> *1st Watchman:* [*indicating Borachio*] This man said, sir, that Don John the prince's brother was a villain.
> *Dogberry:* [*to the sexton*] Write down 'Prince John a villain'. Why, this is flat[1] perjury, to call a prince's brother villain!
> *Borachio:* Master constable –
> *Dogberry:* Pray thee, fellow, peace! I do not like thy look, I promise thee.
> *Sexton:* What heard you him say else?
> *2nd Watchman:* Marry, that he had received a thousand ducats of Don John for accusing the Lady Hero wrongfully.
> *Dogberry:* Flat burglary as ever was committed!
>
> [1] *downright, blatant*

The watchmen also overheard Borachio boast that he had succeeded in persuading Claudio, through his play-acting, to disgrace Hero in church the next day.

The sexton, unlike Dogberry and Verges, realises exactly what has happened. He has heard that Don John has suddenly fled from Messina, and has also been told about Hero's humiliation; he believes, as officially announced, that Hero is dead. Clearly these two men have been involved in a malicious plot:

Sexton: … this is more, masters, than you can deny. Prince John is this morning secretly stolen away; Hero was in this manner[1] accused, in this very manner refused[2] and, upon the grief of this, suddenly died. Master constable, let these men be bound, and brought to Leonato's.

[1] *just as reported by the watchmen*
[2] *rejected, disowned*

The sexton leaves to present his report urgently to Leonato. Meanwhile, the men of the watch tie up the two prisoners. Dogberry is frustrated that the sexton is no longer present to record Conrade's insolence as he struggles to resist his captors:

Dogberry: Come, bind them. Thou naughty varlet!
Conrade: Away! You are an ass, you are an ass!
Dogberry: Dost thou not suspect[1] my place?[2] Dost thou not suspect my years? O, that he were here[3] to write me down an ass! But masters, remember that I am an ass; though it be not written down, yet forget not that I am an ass.

[1] *respect*
[2] *position, authority*
[3] *I wish the sexton were here*

"Dogberry is a great respecter of words – of long words, defaming words, and the phraseology of official regulations – but he respects them only with respect to himself; he interprets the regulations for his own peace of mind and uses words for the little that they mean to himself, not for what they mean to others."

John Russell Brown, *Shakespeare and his Comedies*, 1962

An emotional outburst

Heartbroken at his daughter's suffering, Leonato rejects his brother Antonio's attempts to console him. Only someone who has been through a similar experience can offer any comfort, he believes. Giving abstract advice is easy, but dealing with one's own suffering as a human being is a different matter:

> *Leonato:*   ... I will be flesh and blood.
> For there was never yet philosopher
> That could endure the toothache patiently,
> However they have writ the style of gods [1]
> And made a push at chance and sufferance. [2]
>
> [1] *even if they have written with godlike authority*
> [2] *defiantly rejected misfortune and suffering*

Antonio urges his brother not to punish himself by dwelling on his feelings; instead, he should vent his anger on those who have caused his grief. Leonato agrees. Although his initial reaction in the church was to blame Hero for her deceitfulness, he now suspects that the accusations made by Claudio and Don Pedro were false.

At this moment Hero's two accusers appear. Leonato confronts them, but it is clear that they are in no mood for conflict: the governor is an elderly, respected figure, and Claudio and Don Pedro are unwilling to argue with him. Undeterred, Leonato addresses Claudio aggressively. Unlike Claudio, he is aware that Hero is still alive, but in his indignation he accuses the young man of causing her death:

> *Leonato:*   ... Thou hast so wronged my innocent child and me
> That I am forced to lay my reverence by, [1]
> And with grey hairs and bruise of many days [2]
> Do challenge thee to trial of man. [3]
> I say thou hast belied mine innocent child.
> Thy slander hath gone through and through her heart,
> And she lies buried with her ancestors ...
>
> [1] *put aside the respect that my age usually inspires*
> [2] *the aches and pains of old age*
> [3] *single combat; a duel*

Claudio and Don Pedro refuse to quarrel with the elderly governor, and insist that they have done nothing wrong. Antonio steps forward, offering to take his brother's place and fight the young man. He becomes increasingly heated, hurling insults at Claudio and the prince despite his brother's attempts to restrain him:

Antonio:	Boys, apes, braggarts, jacks, milksops! [1]
Leonato:	Brother Anthony –
Antonio:	Hold you content.[2] What, man? I know them, yea,
	And what they weigh, even to the utmost scruple.[3]
	Scambling, outfacing, fashion-monging boys,[4]
	That lie, and cog, and flout,[5] deprave and slander ...

[1] *louts, cowards*
[2] *be quiet, leave me alone*
[3] *I know what they are like, down to the last detail*
[4] *argumentative, brazen, foppish*
[5] *cheat and jeer*

Remaining calm, Don Pedro tries to withdraw politely from the confrontation. He asserts again that the accusations made against Hero were true:

Don Pedro:	Gentlemen both, we will not wake your patience.[1]
	My heart is sorry for your daughter's death,
	But on my honour she was charged with nothing
	But what was true and very full of proof.[2]

[1] *we will not disturb you any longer*
[2] *completely capable of being proved, irrefutable*

The two brothers leave, still seething with anger.

A parting of the ways

Benedick now approaches. Don Pedro and Claudio, keen to engage in their usual banter, are delighted to see him. They have narrowly avoided a clash with the elderly governor and his brother, they report with amusement. Benedick's response is unexpectedly terse:

Claudio:	We had like to have had[1] our two noses snapped off with[2] two old men without teeth.
Don Pedro:	Leonato and his brother. What think'st thou? Had we fought, I doubt[3] we should have been too young for them.
Benedick:	In a false[4] quarrel there is no true valour.

[1] *came close to having*
[2] *by*
[3] *suspect, fear*
[4] *unnecessary*

Don Pedro and Claudio continue in their light-hearted vein, but it quickly becomes clear to them that their friend is in an unusually serious mood. Uninterested in the others' quick-witted conversation, Benedick takes Claudio aside and delivers his challenge, as promised to Beatrice. His words are solemn and uncompromising:

Benedick:	You are a villain. I jest not. I will make it good[1] how you dare, with what[2] you dare and when you dare. Do me right,[3] or I will protest your cowardice. You have killed a sweet lady, and her death shall fall heavy on you.

[1] *back up my word, fight with you*
[2] *with whatever weapon*
[3] *give me a suitable response, answer my challenge*

When they return, Don Pedro asks what the two of them have been discussing, hoping that they have been invited to a feast. Claudio replies ambivalently, and he and Don Pedro resume their flippant exchanges, teasing Benedick about his feelings for Beatrice.

Ignoring their mockery, Benedick tells Claudio not to forget the challenge he has just given. He then bids Don Pedro a cold, formal farewell. He mentions that the prince's brother has disappeared from Messina, and repeats the charge – though he knows that in truth Hero is alive – that Claudio and Don Pedro are responsible for her death:

Benedick: Boy, you know my mind. I will leave you now to your gossip-like humour. You break jests as braggarts do their blades,[1] which, God be thanked, hurt not. My lord,[2] for your many courtesies, I thank you. I must discontinue your company. Your brother the bastard is fled from Messina; you have among you killed a sweet and innocent lady.

[1] *your witticisms are harmless, like the swords of braggarts who have deliberately broken their blades in order to seem heroic*
[2] *Don Pedro*

> *"Don John arrives with his half-brother Don Pedro and simultaneously they lay their plots in the two halves of the play, Don John to destroy love in the trick he plays on Claudio, Don Pedro to create it in the trick he plays on Benedick. Both, in the process, expose truths deeper than they are aware."*
>
> Levi Fox, *The Shakespeare Handbook*, 1987

An admission of guilt

Don Pedro is taken aback to learn that Benedick has genuinely challenged Claudio to a duel. The news that his brother has fled from Messina has also come as a shock.

Just as Don Pedro is reflecting on the seriousness of these developments, his thoughts are interrupted by the sudden approach of a noisy crowd. Dogberry and Verges now enter, along with the men of the watch and their two captives, tethered with ropes. To his alarm, the prince recognises the two prisoners as his brother's attendants, Conrade and Borachio.

When questioned, Dogberry explains, in his usual disjointed style, why the two men have been apprehended:

> *Don Pedro:* Officers, what offence have these men done?
> *Dogberry:* Marry, sir, they have committed false report.
> Moreover they have spoken untruths, secondarily
> they are slanders, sixth and lastly, they have belied
> a lady, thirdly they have verified unjust things, and,
> to conclude, they are lying knaves.

Unable to make sense of Dogberry's rambling answer, the prince turns directly to the suspects. Like those around him, Borachio believes that Hero is dead, and he now decides to confess everything, without delay and with no attempt to justify his crime. He realises that his trickery has had terrible consequences:

> *Borachio:* … hear me, and let this Count kill me. I have deceived
> even your very eyes. What your wisdoms could not
> discover,[1] these shallow fools have brought to light,
> who in the night overheard me confessing to this man[2]
> how Don John your brother incensed[3] me to slander the
> lady Hero; how you were brought into the orchard and
> saw me court Margaret in Hero's garments …
>
> [1] *what Don Pedro and Claudio, with all their wisdom,*
> *were unable to establish*
> [2] *Conrade*
> [3] *incited, encouraged*

Claudio and Don Pedro realise, with horror, that their accusations were false, and that Hero was innocent:

Borachio: The lady is dead upon mine and my master's false
accusation, and, briefly, I desire nothing but the reward
of a villain.
Don Pedro: Runs not this speech like iron through your blood?
Claudio: I have drunk poison whiles he uttered it.

Don Pedro is appalled at his brother's duplicity. Claudio's first thought, in contrast, is for Hero, who now appears in his mind's eye, innocent and beautiful, just as when he first fell in love with her:

Don Pedro: But did my brother set thee on to this?
Borachio: Yea, and paid me richly for the practice of it.[1]
Don Pedro: He is composed and framed[2] of treachery,
And fled he is upon this villainy.
Claudio: Sweet Hero! Now thy image doth appear
In the rare semblance[3] that I loved it first.

[1] *carrying it out*
[2] *shaped, moulded*
[3] *wonderful form*

Making amends

Dogberry orders the prisoners to be taken away to face the governor; by now, the sexton will have presented him with a written statement. The constable is still smarting from the omission of Conrade's insult from the report:

Dogberry: By this time our sexton hath reformed[1] Signior
Leonato of the matter. And masters, do not forget
to specify, when time and place shall serve, that I
am an ass.

[1] *informed*

At this point the governor himself appears, accompanied by his brother and the sexton. The sexton's report has confirmed, as Leonato already suspected, that his daughter was completely innocent of the alleged infidelity.

Leonato refuses to accept that it was Borachio alone who brought about the catastrophe that befell Hero, and he addresses the two noblemen sarcastically:

Borachio: If you would know your wronger, look on me.
Leonato: Art thou the slave that with thy breath hast killed
Mine innocent child?
Borachio: Yea, even I alone.
Leonato: No, not so, villain, thou beliest thyself.[1]
Here stand a pair of honourable men;
A third is fled that had a hand in it.
I thank you, princes, for my daughter's death;
Record it with your high and worthy deeds.
'Twas bravely done ...

[1] *perjure yourself, give false evidence*

Claudio and Don Pedro humbly acknowledge that they will accept whatever punishment the governor deems necessary. Although they are both full of sorrow and regret, they claim that they were misguided, and not malicious, in their conduct:

Claudio: Choose your revenge yourself,
Impose me to what penance your invention
Can lay upon my sin.[1] Yet sinned I not
But in mistaking.
Don Pedro: By my soul, nor I.
And yet to satisfy this good old man
I would bend under any heavy weight
That he'll enjoin me to.[2]

[1] *subject me to whatever penalty your imagination can devise*
[2] *any punishment that he will determine for me*

Leonato commands them both to make it known throughout Messina that his daughter was innocent. He instructs Claudio to write an epitaph in commemoration of Hero's death, to be placed on her tomb and sung at her graveside this evening.

Leonato now makes a surprising revelation. His brother has a daughter, he says, who is very similar to Hero, and is the only surviving child of the family. If Claudio agrees to marry her, he announces, his wrongdoing will be forgiven. The young man is overcome with gratitude:

Leonato: My brother hath a daughter,
          Almost the copy of my child that's dead,
          And she alone is heir to both of us.
          Give her the right[1] you should have given her cousin,
          And so dies my revenge.
Claudio: O noble sir!
          Your over-kindness doth wring tears from me.
          I do embrace your offer ...

          [1] *rightful respect; marriage vows*

The wedding must take place tomorrow, Leonato stipulates. He then mentions that Margaret, who played the part of Hero in the attempted deception, will be questioned along with the other offenders. Borachio immediately speaks up in her defence:

Leonato: This naughty[1] man
          Shall face to face be brought to Margaret,
          Who I believe was packed[2] in all this wrong,
          Hired to it by your brother.
Borachio: No, by my soul she was not,
          Nor knew not what she did when she spoke to me,
          But always hath been just and virtuous
          In anything that I do know by[3] her.

          [1] *wicked*
          [2] *closely involved, an accomplice*
          [3] *of*

Dogberry interrupts respectfully. He wishes to make it known that the question of Margaret's guilt is not the only outstanding matter:

Dogberry: Moreover, sir, which indeed is not under white and
          black,[1] this plaintiff here, the offender, did call me ass.
          I beseech you let it be remembered in his punishment.

          [1] *in the written report*

Leonato thanks Dogberry and hands him a reward for his efforts. After a lengthy, wordy farewell, the constable hands over the prisoners and, along with Verges, takes his leave.

The news spreads V, ii

Margaret, meanwhile, is with Benedick. He wants her to find Beatrice and ask her to speak with him. Margaret notices that Benedick is writing, and playfully asks for her own sonnet as a reward. She deliberately misunderstands his answer, finding a bawdy double meaning in his words. If she were to live a celibate life, she suggests, she will be a servant for ever:

Margaret:	Will you then write me a sonnet in praise of my beauty?
Benedick:	In so high a style, Margaret, that no man living shall come over[1] it; for in most comely truth thou deservest it.
Margaret:	To have no man come over[2] me? Why, shall I always keep below stairs?[3]
Benedick:	Thy wit is as quick as the greyhound's mouth, it catches.[4]
Margaret:	And yours as blunt as the fencer's foils,[5] which hit, but hurt not.
Benedick:	A most manly wit, Margaret, it will not hurt a woman.

[1] *surpass, exceed*
[2] *have intercourse with*
[3] *remain in the unmarried servants' quarters*
[4] *seizes its prey*
[5] *blunted rapiers*

Margaret leaves, and Benedick returns to his writing. His attempts to write a sonnet to Beatrice are not going well. He is unable to translate his intense feelings into verse, he complains, resigning himself to the fact that writing poetry is simply not in his nature:

Benedick:	I have tried. I can find out no rhyme to 'lady' but 'baby' – an innocent rhyme; for 'scorn', 'horn' – a hard rhyme; for 'school', 'fool' – a babbling rhyme ... No, I was not born under a rhyming planet, nor I cannot woo in festival[1] terms.

[1] *light-hearted, celebratory*

Beatrice now comes to join him. She asks him about Claudio, and Benedick confirms that he has challenged the count to a duel, as he had promised. However, he is more interested in talking about love, and the two of them talk lightly and wittily of their feelings for each other. It is not long, though, before their talk turns to Hero; she is still suffering terribly after her rejection, and Beatrice shares her distress.

Just as Benedick is trying to comfort Beatrice, the conversation is interrupted by the sudden arrival of Hero's attendant Ursula. She reports breathlessly that she has just witnessed an astonishing scene in Leonato's house:

Ursula: Madam, you must come to your uncle. Yonder's old coil[1] at home. It is proved my lady Hero hath been falsely accused, the prince and Claudio mightily abused,[2] and Don John is the author of all, who is fled and gone.

[1] *there's great turmoil*
[2] *deceived*

Eager to hear more, Benedick and Beatrice hurry to the governor's house.

... Don John is the author of all, who is fled and gone.

"The villain is still at large ... Perhaps more disconcertingly though, the word 'author' might remind us that it is not Don John, but Shakespeare who planned the deceptions in the play. Theatre itself is implicated in the many false shows we've witnessed ... we were lulled into believing that we could see beyond the costumes. But as the play draws to a close, it's hard to feel so confident that we can tell proof from performance."

Andrea Varney, *Deception and Dramatic Irony in Much Ado About Nothing*, 2016

Remembrance

It is late at night. Claudio has come, by candlelight, to Leonato's family tomb. Don Pedro is with him, along with attendants and musicians. As he promised Leonato, Claudio has brought a scroll on which he has written an epitaph for Hero, which he now recites:

> *Done to death by slanderous tongues*
> *Was the Hero that here lies;*
> *Death, in guerdon of her wrongs,[1]*
> *Gives her fame which never dies;*
> *So the life that died with shame,*
> *Lives in death with glorious fame.*

[1] *as recompense for the wrongs done to her*

Claudio hangs the scroll on the tomb, and instructs the musicians to sing as he and Don Pedro circle the grave in penance. Their hymn is to Diana, virgin goddess of the moon, asking for her forgiveness:

> *Pardon, goddess of the night,*
> *Those that slew thy virgin knight,[1]*
> *For the which, with songs of woe,*
> *Round about her tomb they go.*
> *Midnight, assist our moan,*
> *Help us to sigh and groan ...*

[1] *your devoted follower; Hero*

Claudio vows that this ritual will be carried out every year in commemoration of Hero's death.

Morning is approaching. It is time for them to leave, and change from their funeral garb into festive clothes: today Claudio will be marrying his unknown bride.

A revelation

The atmosphere in Leonato's house is lively and cheerful. The friar, who has come to conduct Claudio's wedding, is discussing recent events with Leonato, his brother Antonio and Benedick.

The friar suspected from the start that Hero was innocent, and is delighted to have been proved right. Leonato reveals that Margaret, though involved in the deception, was not aware of the significance of her play-acting as Hero. For his part, Benedick is glad that the threatened confrontation will not now take place:

Antonio:	Well, I am glad that all things sort[1] so well.
Benedick:	And so am I, being else by faith enforced[2]
	To call young Claudio to a reckoning[3] for it.

[1] *have turned out, ended up*
[2] *bound by my promise*
[3] *settling of accounts; a duel*

Hero and Beatrice are present too, along with Ursula and Margaret. As Claudio and Don Pedro are due to arrive shortly, Leonato asks the ladies to leave the room; when they return they are all to wear masks.

Benedick cautiously approaches the subject of his feelings for Beatrice. He will need the friar's assistance, he mentions, as well as the goodwill of Leonato, as Beatrice's uncle and guardian. Leonato refers knowingly to the part that others have played in bringing the two of them together, remembering the carefully staged conversations in the garden:

Benedick:	Friar, I must entreat your pains,[1] I think.
Friar:	To do what, signior?
Benedick:	To bind me, or undo me,[2] one of them.
	Signior Leonato – truth it is, good signior,
	Your niece regards me with an eye of favour.
Leonato:	That eye my daughter lent her? 'Tis most true.
Benedick:	And I do with an eye of love requite her.[3]

| Leonato: | The sight whereof I think you had from me, |
| | From Claudio and the prince. |

¹ *ask for your help*
² *to bind me in marriage – or possibly ruin my life*
³ *return her feelings*

The friar readily agrees to carry out the wedding, and Leonato, equally enthusiastic, gives his blessing.

Claudio and Don Pedro now arrive. Leonato asks Claudio again whether he is prepared to marry the bride who has been chosen for him. The young man promises that he will keep his word, and Antonio brings in the four masked women.

Claudio, presented with his new bride, asks to see her face, but Leonato insists that he must first make his marriage vow. Claudio agrees, and is stunned and overjoyed to see his beloved back from the dead:

Claudio:	Give me your hand before this holy friar.
	I am your husband, if you like of me.
Hero:	[*removing her mask*] And when I lived I was your
	other wife;
	And when you loved, you were my other husband.
Claudio:	Another Hero!
Hero:	Nothing certainer.
	One Hero died defiled,¹ but I do live,
	And surely as I live, I am a maid.
Don Pedro:	The former Hero! Hero that is dead!
Leonato:	She died, my lord, but whiles² her slander lived.

¹ *dishonoured, vilified*
² *only as long as*

I am your husband, if you like of me.

"In prejudiced blindness to Hero's true nature Claudio rejected her; enlightened, in humble and penitent trust, he accepts her supposed substitute."

A. R. Humphreys, Introduction to the Arden
Shakespeare edition of *Much Ado About Nothing*, 1981

The friar promises Claudio and the prince that everything will be explained in due course. Now, however, they are all to move on to the chapel; it is time for the wedding.

Benedick has the last word

Benedick interrupts proceedings to address Beatrice. At first, they cannot bring themselves to make a public declaration of their love:

> *Benedick:* Do you not love me?
> *Beatrice:*   Why, no, no more than reason.
> *Benedick:* Why then your uncle and the prince and Claudio
> Have been deceived – they swore you did.
> *Beatrice:* Do you not love me?
> *Benedick:*   Troth[1] no, no more than reason.
>
> [1] *in truth*

They repeat some of the extravagant claims that others have made about their feelings for one another. Now, however, both maintain that they wish only to be good friends. Leonato urges Beatrice to admit how she really feels, and Claudio produces conclusive proof of Benedick's devotion. His unsuccessful attempts at poetry have come to light:

> *Leonato:* Come, cousin,[1] I am sure you love the gentleman.
> *Claudio:* And I'll be sworn upon't that he loves her,
> For here's a paper written in his hand,
> A halting[2] sonnet of his own pure brain[3]
> Fashioned to Beatrice.
>
> [1] *niece; Beatrice*
> [2] *clumsy, inept*
> [3] *purely of his own composition*

Hero presents a similar love-poem, stolen from Beatrice's pocket, dedicated to Benedick. The two of them can no longer maintain their pretence that they are simply friends. Although they agree to marry, however, each now claims to be motivated purely by sympathy for the other's suffering. Leonato, determined to put an end to the couple's denials and evasions, calls on them to be silent.

He brings the two of them closer and, to the delight of onlookers, they embrace:

Benedick: A miracle! Here's our own hands against our hearts.[1] Come, I will have thee, but by this light I take thee for pity.

Beatrice: I would not deny you, but by this good day I yield upon great persuasion – and partly to save your life, for I was told you were in a consumption.[2]

Leonato: Peace! [*bringing Beatrice and Benedick together*] I will stop your mouth.

[1] *our own handwriting betraying our deepest feelings*
[2] *wasting away, pining*

Don Pedro teases Benedick for finally succumbing to marriage despite his earlier pledges to remain single. Benedick cheerfully shrugs off the prince's remarks. He has changed his mind, and that is that:

Benedick: I'll tell thee what, Prince; a college of wit-crackers cannot flout me out of my humour.[1] Dost thou think I care for a satire or an epigram? ... In brief, since I do purpose[2] to marry, I will think nothing to any purpose[3] that the world can say against it; and therefore never flout at me for what I have said against it. For man is a giddy[4] thing, and this is my conclusion.

[1] *cannot change my mind with mockery*
[2] *intend*
[3] *I won't take any notice of anything*
[4] *changeable, capricious*

... I will stop your mouth.

"We finally get the kiss that we've been waiting for. But its connotation is ambiguous: Beatrice's mouth is literally stopped – she doesn't say a word after this. Benedick talks on to the play's end, very much taking his place as the newly dominant male ..."

Penny Gay, *Benedick and Beatrice: the 'merry war' of courtship*, 2016

It is time to dance, announces Benedick. Leonato protests that the weddings must take place first, but Benedick is adamant, and calls out for the musicians to play. In passing, he turns to Don Pedro: it is now the prince's turn to get married, he exclaims heartily.

Before the dancing can start, a messenger rushes in with dramatic news, and a hush falls over the party:

> *Messenger:* My lord, your brother John is ta'en in flight [1]
> And brought with armed men back to Messina.
>
> [1] *captured while he was attempting to escape*

Benedick refuses to let thoughts of the villainous Don John dampen the spirits of the assembled guests. They have survived his malicious plans, and can worry about his punishment later. Benedick assures the prince that he will come up with something:

> *Benedick:* Think not on him till tomorrow; I'll devise thee brave [1]
> punishments for him. Strike up, pipers!
>
> [1] *fine, worthy*

The music starts up once more. Tragedy has been averted, and harmony restored; and spirits are high as the two couples dance into their bright future.

———
———

What does the future hold for Beatrice and Benedick? Many critics, past and present, have been unable to resist the temptation to predict how married life will work out for the fictional couple.

"On the whole, we dismiss Benedick and Beatrice to their matrimonial bonds rather with a sense of amusement than a feeling of congratulation or sympathy; rather with an acknowledgement that they are well-matched, and worthy of each other, than with any well-founded expectation of their domestic tranquillity."

Anna Brownell Jameson, *Characteristics of Women: Moral, Poetical, and Historical*, 1832

"I have no misgivings about the future happiness of Benedick and Beatrice ... They will always be finding out something new and interesting in each other's character ... She will prove the fitness of her name as Beatrice (the giver of happiness), and he will be glad to confess himself blest indeed in having won her."

Helen Faucit, *On Some of Shakespeare's Female Characters*, 1891

"Perhaps there is just a hint that like most Shakespeare marriages, the union of Beatrice and Benedick may not be a bower of bliss. In this comedy, more than ever, that does not matter. Two of the most intelligent and energetic of Shakespeare's nihilists, neither of them likely to be outraged or defeated, will take their chances together."

Harold Bloom, *Shakespeare: The Invention of the Human*, 1998

"Is the silencing of the play's witty female character the final, mutual expression of romantic fulfilment? Or is it a more coercive or ominous gesture about Beatrice's future role in her marriage?"

Emma Smith, *Comedy, tragedy and gender politics in* Much Ado About Nothing, 2016

Acknowledgements

The following publications have proved invaluable as sources of factual information and critical insight:

- Charles Baskervill, *The Quarrel of Benedick and Beatrice*, from *A Memorial Volume to Shakespeare*, University of Texas Press, 1917

- Jonathan Bate, *Soul of the Age*, Penguin, 2009

- Jonathan Bate, Introduction to the RSC Shakespeare edition of *Much Ado About Nothing*, Macmillan, 2009

- Harold Bloom, *Shakespeare: The Invention of the Human*, HarperCollins, 1998

- Charles Boyce, *Shakespeare A to Z*, Roundtable Press, 1990

- John Russell Brown, *Shakespeare and his Comedies*, Methuen, 1968

- David Daniell, *Shakespeare and the traditions of comedy*, from *The Cambridge Companion to Shakespeare Studies*, Cambridge University Press, 1986

- Terry Eagleton, *William Shakespeare*, Blackwell, 1986

- Alison Findlay, *Women in Shakespeare*, Bloomsbury, 2014

- Nicholas Fogg, *Hidden Shakespeare*, Amberley, 2013

- Levi Fox, *The Shakespeare Handbook*, Bodley Head, 1987

- Penny Gay, *Benedick and Beatrice: the 'merry war of' courtship*, from *Discovering Literature*, British Library, 2016

- John Gielgud, *An Actor and His Time*, Rowman & Littlefield, 1997

- Harold C. Goddard, *The Meaning of Shakespeare*, University of Chicago Press, 1951

- A. R. Humphreys, Introduction to the Arden Shakespeare edition of *Much Ado About Nothing*, Methuen, 1981

- Lisa Jardine, *Rank and Courtship*, from programme notes for *Much Ado About Nothing*, Royal Shakespeare Theatre, 1990

- Holly Kelsey, *Pestilence and Playwright*, Shakespeare Birthplace Trust, 2016

- Claire McEachern, Introduction to the Arden Shakespeare edition of *Much Ado About Nothing*, Bloomsbury, 2016

- Emma Smith, *Comedy, tragedy and gender politics in* Much Ado About Nothing, from *Discovering Literature*, British Library, 2016

- Gary Taylor, *Reinventing Shakespeare*, Hogarth Press, 1989

- Andrea Varney, *Deception and dramatic irony in* Much Ado About Nothing, from *Discovering Literature*, British Library, 2016

- Michael Wood, *In Search of Shakespeare*, BBC Books, 2005

Guides currently available in the *Shakespeare Handbooks* series are:

www.shakespeare-handbooks.com

www.ingramcontent.com/pod-product-compliance
Lightning Source LLC
Chambersburg PA
CBHW071828020426
42331CB00007B/1647